The Improper Opinion

Westminster Studies in Christian Communication
Kendig Brubaker Cully, General Editor

The
Improper
Opinion

Mass Media and the Christian Faith

MARTIN E. MARTY

THE WESTMINSTER PRESS
Philadelphia

To

SIEGFRIED and HARRIET REINHARDT
whose communication in the arts
" is the servant of God to help
his sorrowful creatures, to give
them joy worthy of their destiny."

Contents

A Note on Westminster Studies
in Christian Communication

These Studies are predicated on the ground that the Christian faith needs to be made relevant to persons in the modern world in terms of the dynamic nature of the faith itself and the channels that are capable of conveying such a faith. In itself any technique of communication conceivably could serve as well for secular as for religious ends. In this series a wide variety of means and methods of communication will be analyzed in the light of their availability to, and suitability for, the particular tasks that the Christian church faces in bringing the realities of faith to bear upon the life of actual persons in the contemporary situation.

Oftentimes in the past, techniques have been viewed almost as ends in themselves. Or, they have been taken over uncritically from the secular culture without being subjected to adequate scrutiny as to whether they are appropriate for the church's use. On the other hand, sometimes the church has been blind to the life situations of the present to such an extent as to ignore the real ways in which people's lives are influenced by all that impinges on them. In the latter case, the church has failed to bring the life-giving power of the gospel to bear on contemporary culture because of a lack of understanding of, or appreciation for, the means of communication that have been proved capable of changing lives and societies.

Involving as it does both the " What " and the " How," the whole question of the communication of the gospel in the modern world is pivotal in the present juncture of history. Starting with these initial volumes, the present Studies will be aimed at bringing the " What " and the " How " together fruitfully. These books are designed to make a contribution to the ongoing conversations across boundaries. Theology, Biblical studies, sociology, cultural anthropology, psychology, education, art, letters, science, and the other disciplines, all have something to say to one another. In our present concern, "communication" refers to the way in which the Christian faith can come into conjunction with what is happening in the total world of life and ideas in the middle decades of the twentieth century. In each of these Studies attention will focus on some important aspect of the basic question: How can the church most effectively preach, teach, and otherwise manifest the gospel in the growing edges of man's present-day culture? No aspect of man's actual situation is alien to such a question. No medium of communication should fail to come under scrutiny if, as Christians, we are eager to have the Word of God confront a confused generation powerfully and compellingly.

Each volume in Westminster Studies in Christian Communication will be an authentic voice of one perceptive interpreter. No effort has been made to suggest to any writer what "line" he ought to follow. Each work will be adjudged by the readers on its own merits. The writers themselves conceivably might disagree heartily with regard to certain presuppositions or conclusions held by their colleagues. All this will be to the good if the result of these Studies should be the stimulating of many conversations. Yet all the writers have in mind a focus that is realistic, an emphasis that is practical, and a discussion that is timely. The only request made of the authors is that they speak out of their knowledge to the very heart and mind of our times. Depth without dullness, breadth without diffuseness, challenge without sentimentality — these, at least, it is hoped, will be characteristic of all the Studies. We are grateful to those who have consented to share in this venture into communication, and we commend their work as in itself an integral part of the church's task of communication.

KENDIG BRUBAKER CULLY
General Editor

Evanston, Illinois

Acknowledgments

Parts of this material were delivered as lectures at Gettysburg College, Gettysburg, Pennsylvania; at Des Moines, Iowa, to the ministerium of the American Evangelical Lutheran Church; at Washington, D.C., in a lectureship sponsored jointly by the Department of Religion of Howard University and the National Capitol Area Council of Churches. I thank my hosts on these three occasions as well as the unusually responsive audiences whose comments and contributions are incorporated in these developing themes. They have given me the confidence to present this work to a wider audience. Dr. Kendig Brubaker Cully motivated and guided the project from its inception; Cecilia Gaul edited the copy; Mrs. Florence Adam typed the manuscripts. I thank them too.

MARTIN E. MARTY

Chicago, Illinois

Preface

The presentation of the Christian faith in a world significantly shaped by mass media of communication is a task that concerns the whole church. It would be misleading to direct discussion of this topic only to those responsible for communicating. Authors of best-selling books, publishers of magazines and newspapers, and producers of motion pictures, radio, and television programs will, if they are Christian, have this concern at heart. But the mass conversion of producers, writers, and directors would not begin to solve the complex of problems that new forms of expression have placed before the whole church. Therefore, this book is directed to people who read books, magazines, and newspapers; to those whose own values are shaped in part by motion pictures, radio, and television.

One in a series of studies in communication, this book will not use that word as often as it will "presentation" of the Christian faith. This word is more faithful to expression through mass media (which is essentially monologue) and has a more precise theological bearing. Much as it is a study of the faith and the media, it is also concerned with the people who are involved with both. More, it asks questions concerning a fuller Christian ministry in an age when these media dominate public discourse. Finally, it includes some interest in Christian strategy in such an age.

Lest what may seem the pretensions of that paragraph carry

us away we can issue some disclaimers. This is not a technical study of the nature of the media. Such studies exist in abundance and they are being added to constantly by engineers, critics, and sociologists. Although informed by their work and in no way detracting from its legitimacy, I am not seeking to make a contribution in realms beyond my disciplines or competence, as such a technical subject would be. Nor is this a sociological study of the impact of the media on people at different times and in different places. This topic is closer to the subject, but it implies the use of other kinds of data and methods to achieve a different goal. And it is not an exercise in criticism from any particular aesthetic point of view, though I consider expression in these media as much an art as a science. Again and again aesthetic judgments may appear in passing, and throughout I shall suggest that the Christian faith dare never settle for a second-best artistically; but these judgments are secondary to the main purpose.

In place of these, this book brings together a historical study of the recent past and present cultural setting with a Christian theological inquiry that has been informed by the more technical studies of the media. It is an attempt at reasoned and, I hope, reasonable discourse about a subject that concerns us all and that concerns me as historian, journalist, and pastor. From the outset, let it be clear that I am an enthusiastic participant in the world that is so significantly determined by the media in question. I have tried always to avoid falling under one of my teacher's strictures: that some of us regard the periodicals Scripturally and the Scriptures periodically. But the fascination of books, magazines, and newspapers never seems to die for me, and to a lesser extent, I am among those who have oftentimes permitted motion pictures, radio, and television to work their spell almost to narcotic effect.

No reader need fear, then, that this discourse comes from one who looks condescendingly on all forms of popular culture. Viewing the resplendence of Christian opportunities in a critical age, I confess that I am ashamed of Eliseo Vivas for his observation that to be ashamed of having been born into the twentieth century is a mark of human decency. The twentieth century produces the mature mass media of communication as it was produced so largely by them; as an age, a situation, or an intellectual construct we cannot escape it, and the attempt to do so through shame or condescension is not particularly creative.

If there is one inclusive context for what follows, call it mission history. I like to see the question of presenting the Christian faith in our time constantly and almost compulsively in missionary terms. The retreat of the churches, the rollback of their empires, the withdrawal of their claims, the slackening of their hold on people is sufficiently marked to make the entire world — including the West — missionary territory. Words written or spoken, images formed, hopes made incandescent in such a time, are worthless and wasted if they do not keep this reconciling purpose in view.

The reconciling message of God's activity in Jesus Christ is the same from age to age. It has outlasted and sometimes outwitted competition in other times and other places. It would be heard again by people in need in this age of mass media and mass men. But there are " other voices, other rooms."

Proper and Improper Opinions

Our researchers into Public Opinion are content
That he held the proper opinions for the time of
year.
— W. H. AUDEN's " UNKNOWN CITIZEN."

But God chose what is foolish in the world to
shame the wise,
God chose what is weak in the world to shame
the strong.
— PAUL's " UNKNOWN CITIZEN," I COR. 1:27.

Introduction:
The World of Mass Media

The twenty-fifth of the celebrated letters of Screwtape, the archdevil, to his nephew Wormwood[1] gives fair warning against combining Christianity with the latest vogues. Lewis waggishly pokes fun at faddism in the name of faith in this satanic inversion:

My dear Wormwood,

The real trouble about the set your patient is living in is that it is *merely* Christian. They all have individual interests, of course, but the bond remains mere Christianity. What we want, if men become Christians at all, is to keep them in the state of mind I call " Christianity And." You know — Christianity and the Crisis, Christianity and the New Psychology, Christianity and the New Order, Christianity and Faith Healing, Christianity and Psychical Research, Christianity and Vegetarianism, Christianity and Spelling Reform. If they must be Christians, let them at least be Christians with a difference. Substitute for the faith itself some Fashion with a Christian colouring. Work on their horror of the Same Old Thing.

Screwtape might as well have added " Christianity and Mass Media of Communication." At this late date we all know that it has become fashionable to make much of communication and to make fun of those who make much of it. We know that the mass media interest the mass. Bring these into connection with Christianity at a time when religion finds favor in a nation, and you have an unbeatable combination. This tendency to be patronizing about contemporary concerns during their hour of fashion, however, does not relieve us of responsibility in relation to them. If we could honestly claim that we have made a first step in effectively encountering the world that is spellbound by the public media, we could dismiss the subject with a bored shrug, a knowing smile. Such a luxury is not granted us.

In face of the temptation to be voguish and timely and the parallel temptation to avoid the timely because of sophistication, we can take measures to counteract the dangers. For my part, I will attempt to do this by removing whatever traces of sensationalism might creep in while discussing the books, articles, or images that this subject evokes. It is not difficult to prepare a quotable criticism of Hollywood's failures and the eccentricities of the Publishers' Rows. There must also be room, however, for an approach that is not so readily dated or so shrill and strident. The attempt to see the media in a larger cultural and theological context will be a partial safeguard here.

If we urge the necessity of this subject, there is again the hazard of its being greeted with the yawn of a Christian world that is weary of hearing " Crisis! " so often. The faith has outlasted onslaughts more bold and sudden than anything in the value-systems accompanying modern expression. Must we roll over and play dead because another author is obsessed with another crisis in Christian expression? There is warrant for this reserve, and yet there is warrant for pointing to ways in which the mass media present a problem that is new both in its quantity and in its quality.

For a sample, begin by seeing the mass media as a stage in, if not the fruition of, the process of secularization of the West. Not only are these media the product of an industrial, urban, and technical civilization that is secular in most of its bearings, but they also serve as effective means of propagating secular values. Yet secularization by itself is manifestly a containable problem. The church has contended before with men and with generations whose ultimate concerns seemed bound to the saeculum, the order of the age. As a matter of fact, Christianity was born into such a world, for the Roman religion that it encountered in so many places was but a tired and hollow form. It was called a religion, but it was more a genius of government, an attachment to the imperial office. It conveyed a sense of mystery or transcendence. And in this secular world Christianity made its way so effectively that in two centuries the secular order was itself overturned and the Christian faith became the religion of the Roman Empire.

Secularism and secularization by themselves, then, hold no ultimate terrors for Christians. Parallel this religious and intellectual setting with some physical factors in our time, and again we see fronts that militate against Christianity. Certainly there can be nothing so crucial in the world of mass media to thwart against the Christian possibility as there is, for example, in the demographic explosion. While the Christian world reproduces at a measured pace, the non-Christian world is growing in such a way that statistically Christendom is rendered insignificant. Cannot we reserve " Crisis! " for this predicament? Or one might argue that mobility serves to jostle Christian strategies. Transportation has changed as dramatically as communication, and people are on the move. Growth, crowding, migration, movement — these make nurture and evangelization difficult. Yet Christianity has survived and even profited from previous disruptions, from migrations and crusades of earlier times.

Even more unsettling and more apparently entitled to the term " crucial " is the inhuman potential of modern warfare and scientific weapons. This represents something new to militate against Christians with their gospel of love and peace, it is said. In a sense this question scarcely meets the others on their terms, for if some horror is unleashed here, it would have an annihilating effect, and the talk that preceded it would have been vain babbling. So we must say that, when reduced to a human scale, this problem is not qualitatively new. Joseph Stalin once said that the death of a million people is a statistic, but the death of one person is a tragedy. In the tragic sense Christians have faced annihilation of peoples and races in many times and places. They have known plagues and decimating illnesses, wars of extermination and annihilating experiences, even if the boundaries and extents were limited. This is all, then, a horror in a different class, but it is not wholly new.

Taking its place with the intellectual and physical disruptions of the time are psychic violations of integrity and balance that also lead to new anxieties for Christians. People are bewildered by the break-throughs in science, education, history, and art. They are lost, having a vague sense of destiny. These changes are different, but not really new; every age presents Christianity with a different world view.

So the crisis presented to Christian proclamation and nurture by mass media of communication is in some ways unique; it has less precedent in earlier Christian experience. The mass media are, first of all, the means by which all the other intellectual, physical, and psychic jars and jolts seem to be brought home to people. And they have a peculiarly subtle potential: they create the illusion that "business is as usual" while massive and pervasive change is taking place. Because Christianity brings with it ideas and values surrounding the Person at its center, and because these are upstaged by other ideas and values on all fronts at all times in all ways (we must be permitted slight exaggeration to suggest the Protean character of the media), this challenge is still new and the outcome uncertain, the faith untried.

Artificial communication to numbers of people is, of course, ancient. The primeval orator who mounted a rock and declaimed to the masses in the valley before a battle was indulging in mass communications, with his larynx as the medium. The sound of drums or the signaling with smoke that we associate with primitive societies represent effective means of mass communication, despite the limits these means place on articulateness. All these fall short of the distinctly modern conception that has shrunk the world and shown itself to have a decisive influence in forming opinion and attitude. It is only during the last half millennium and even more during the last half century that the idea of instant, total, dramatic impact on the lives of millions by a communicator has matured.

To see the process in action, and to chronicle the change it means for a community such as the universal Christian church, we do well to notice the increase in pace of production and distribution that have come with the passing of time. For the sake of convenience we shall concentrate on six forms of communication; each successively represents an increase in pace, dynamic, and impermanence over the earlier development. The statistics that follow depict the situation in round numbers as it obtained in America in the latter years of the 1950's.

First of all, books. Over thirteen thousand titles were printed annually, with production running to over six hundred million copies. These commercial ventures were the effort of hundreds of publishers, yet power is concentrated in a few. Thirty publishers marketed 60 per cent of the books and one hundred published 85 per cent of the year's output. Three fourths of a billion dollars went into the purchase of these books. This sum represents a relatively small factor in the American economy, but its smallness is in part a reflection again of the relatively low cost per item.

The book as we know it is conventionally thought of as having been born with the development of movable type late in the fifteenth century. The effective use of this invention in forming opinion became clear as early as the sixteenth century, when humanist ideas and the influences of the Reformation were spread on the Continent and in England through tract, pamphlet, and book. It is difficult today to picture the dramatic influence of this relatively undeveloped medium in its time; theses and dissertations that strike us as being very limited in scope and very ponderous in subject and manner seemed to spread in brush-fire fashion.

For the succeeding three centuries the pamphlet, monograph, or book was the chief medium for marketing or presenting ideas beyond the local area. A change of pace came with the development of production methods after the Industrial Revolution and the improvement in transportation methods after the middle of the nineteenth century. These led to two phenomena that are of recent origin, the best seller and the paperback in its modern form. The best seller is a book obviously designed for mass consumption and ordinarily predictably salable. It comes from the pen of a colorful or even charismatic figure; it treats themes that appeal to the insecurities, the hopes, or the passions of large numbers of people; it is easily advertised and highly marketable. In the sense that a book must compete with other media, the best seller stands alone. Almost as soon as it is off the press it is on the coffee tables of hundreds of thousands of book-club members, is condensed in newspapers, is discussed and debated. Only such a book can really be classified as a mass medium, as most of the authors of the annual thirteen thousand titles are ruefully aware. The development since World War II on an international scale of books of varying quality and appeal in less expensive paper covers has made possible mass distribution and mass marketing for numbers of books that were once imprisoned between forbidding hard covers and behind forbidding high prices. It is this phase of book-publishing that has made possible the display of *Faust* or *The Odyssey* on the same rack with the sex novel at corner drugstores and bus stations across America. This trend represents the general direction of mass media saturation: an increase in pace and the look of impermanence. But even it is relatively static; a book makes greater demands on the person whom the communicator desires to reach than do most of the other media.

A second phase of publishing the printed page appears with the mass magazine market. Here again we have a development that has roots in the tract and pamphlet of the sixteenth century; it merely represents a regularization of pamphleteering in its earlier forms. By the end of the 1950's over twenty magazines in the United States had a circulation of more than one million each. Over six thousand magazines were being produced, but again there was concentration of power in the five or six largest publishing houses. A one-billion-dollar item in the national economy results from magazine distribution.

With the magazine we have a development in pace and impermanence from the time when scholarly journals represented the leisurely parading of ideas — books in sequence, as it were — to the modern picture or digest magazine, where instant and total impact must be made within minutes on a person casually leafing through it in a dentist's waiting room. The journal was made to be treasured; the magazine is designed to be thrown away. One year's accumulation of a weekly picture magazine would take up more space than most households provide for books.

A third use of the printed page became truly mass communication only with the development of modern industrial communities, of rapid engraving, typesetting, and gravure processes, and of improved transportation facilities. This is the newspaper, whose long and distinguished history as molder of opinions and inspirer of activity needs no documentation. At the time of this writing there were over seventeen hundred daily newspapers in the United States (and almost eighty-five hundred weeklies) producing fifty-six million copies per day and totaling three to four billion dollars in the annual economy. A definite trend toward concentration of power is appearing here too, as in city after city newspapers merge or disappear for economic reasons. An example of the way in which the opinion former holds power is the fact that about 70 per cent of the economic basis of newspapers resides in advertising and only about 30 per cent in circulation, which represents the reader's investment.

The newspaper is (if we except the billboard, I suppose) the ultimate in the increase of pace toward impermanence in the use of printing. To call something " as dated as yesterday's newspaper" has become proverbial. But today the newspaper has its hour in shaping the proper opinions among millions of readers.

Some students of communication believe that the logical development of this increasingly ephemeral character of print, the production of reading matter designed to be skimmed or casually observed and then discarded, the publishing of material for instant and unthinking response, is a harbinger of the end of the age of Gutenberg. Along this line of argument, although there would always be room for the printed page, it will lose its decisiveness because it is being outpaced by other media that demand even less of the person involved with them. These are the media that are occasioned less by the verbal than by the visual or aural possibilities. The forms of communication that are part of this second phase permit less selectivity on the part of the viewer or listener, and as such are put to better use by the propagandizer. They are more dynamic, producing nearly overpowering instantaneous effects on masses.

Before these media could be developed, a series of inventions that are of more recent origin than movable type and the printing press had to come into being. Among these were the vacuum tube and later the transistor, film, artificial sources of light, cameras. After these came motion pictures, radio, and television.

The motion picture, whose years of most massive impact may already be behind us, was developed around the turn of this century and became a subject of popular fascination from the start. Although two-dimensional in character and silent at first, the motion picture brought the dramatic arts and colorful personalities to thousands of communities that were not being reached by the stage. The introduction of sound late in the 1920's brought to maturity this modern medium; its effect on the morals and manners of the nation were immediately apparent. A change in fashion that originated in Paris or Hollywood would be shown weeks later in What Cheer, Iowa, and in America's Middletowns, where they could be copied and

adopted by people of varying means. Sectionalisms and isola-
tionisms were battered and broken by this cross-sectional
medium.

By the later years of the 1950's the weekly audience at movies
approached forty-five million people, though the number of
studios fluctuated widely in a competitive economy. Around
1957 there were over one hundred studios, six of them producing the majority of the successful films that were shown in
eighteen thousand theaters to revenues of over one billion dollars annually.

The motion picture was still somewhat limited as a mass
medium, however, in that it still demanded congregating centers. These, it is true, became ultimately mobile with the development of the drive-in theater. But one still had to get up
and go to the " movies "; of much greater use to communicators
were media that reached people everywhere and at all times.
The first of these pervasive aural media was the radio, of even
more recent development than moving pictures. Although only
0.7 billion of the economy was represented in radio each year
during the later 1950's, radio reached near-saturation as there
were over one hundred million receiving sets in the nation.
Over three thousand stations, ordinarily representing the influence of three or four large networks, furnished opinion and
entertainment. Radio, in some ways recessive as an opinion-
maker with the presence of its successor television for competition, also represents some reversal of the power trend. For
a variety of reasons the network system was less powerful than
it became with the advent of television, and radio tended to
become more and more a regional marketing medium. There
has been an accompanying trend toward the trivialization of
radio on the local level, where popular music is the staple
fare almost the entire broadcasting day.

Radio was the first real " back of the mind " medium, which
could be played while the listener went about other activities.
To millions of housewives, radio accompanied every duty of
the day, seldom obtruding but constantly intruding with a

subtle pattern of values. The radio, in portable form, at bedsides, in autos, made possible the marketing of product and idea to large numbers of people at relatively small expense, and in its heyday during the 1930's it competed with movies as shaper of manners and morals.

Much of the security of earlier media has been jostled by television, which in the decade following World War II burgeoned into first place in impact and influence in the popular mind; tens of millions of sets were added each year to the nation's homes. Well over one billion dollars of the economy were dependent on television. Statistics in this field are unreliable because of the suddenness of change; nor is lengthy discussion of scope and impact necessary, because most people when they hear the term "mass media" today tend to equate it with television. Suffice to say that television brings up to the moment the combination of visual and aural response, is the most comprehensive and the most subtly pervasive of all the media. In many ways it symbolizes the passing of some earlier influences.

Television has been regarded with almost messianic fervor by its partisans and as a satanic delusion by its detractors. Robert Sarnoff of National Broadcasting Company has written:

> When I consider our growing population, the increasing complexity of our society, and the absolute need for reaching, informing, and serving these mushrooming millions so that our government and our economy may function with reasonable cohesion, then I sometimes think the mass media may have been preordained as a unifying force in this era of turbulent growth.[2]

As space developments make possible instantaneous worldwide broadcasting, we see the latest point of maturity in mass communications as a fruition of an industrial, urban, and technical culture that permits considerable leisure time.

From the first, Christians have realized the possibilities to which media of communication and persuasion could be put to present the Christian faith. We have already referred to the part the Reformation played in developing the use of the printed page. But this book is not devoted particularly to the private use of mass media on the part of the churches. Perhaps the best word to use is "broadcast": we are concerned with media that spread their messages broadcast, without selecting audiences. To make the distinction clear, permit me to illustrate.

We are not interested here in the religious novel printed by the denominational press. Because of a relatively captive audience and effective promotional means, such a novel may reach significant circulation. But the influence is felt almost exclusively within the denomination or group concerned: it would be difficult to recall one title of significance that made its way beyond the circle here described. So, in the field of books, we are interested only in the presentation of the Christian faith in what would normally be termed the secular market.

Christian leaders have shown impressive ability, secondly, in copying the methods of magazine production at their best. The readers of the religious "slick" magazines of denominational orientation need not be ashamed of the technical competence or the quality of production of the magazines they place on their coffee tables. Although the presentation of the faith may sometimes be blunted in them, these periodicals reach circulations that approach the highest subscription lists of secular magazines. But, again, they are quite limited. A magazine sent to a million homes of The Methodist Church has a tremendous potential but it is not broadcast. It has a selective audience.

Interest groups in the churches often produce newspapers; some of them, for example *The Christian Science Monitor*, lose enough of their denominational orientation to become competitive dailies in the mass communications field and thus deserve consideration here. But the Roman Catholic diocesan newspapers, no matter how enormous their circulation, or the weekly and monthly press of Protestant groups, still are not technically mass media, however efficiently they borrow the techniques.

For many years religious groups have produced motion pictures, some of them of excellent quality. Only rarely, however, does one of these break the circle of house-organ origin and selected audience to make its way into the commercial theater. Some religious groups, particularly universities and seminaries or missionary training schools, own and operate licensed radio stations. Some of the more creative broadcasting today, particularly in the realm of discussion and classical music, is presented over these. But they drop from our consideration now because we are interested in the world shaped by mass media, and these stations have little appeal beyond their subsidizing and supporting circle. The expenses of television have made it of more limited use as a captive — and I use the word without wanting to load it — of specific religious groups or promotions.

What does interest us is the part that the secular order, the religious world, and the Christian faith play in best-selling books, in popular magazines, in metropolitan newspapers; in commercial motion pictures and over regular and possibly network radio and television. Here is where the decisive molding of popular and proper opinions on its massive scale goes on.

Now if we ask, as a last preliminary, why men desire to communicate to masses of people, we arrive at a cluster of answers. Most of them can be classified along three lines.

Ideas and Ideologies. There is no reason to be crass or cynical and to assume that all ideas are presented for commercial reasons or in order to subjugate the integrity of others. Ideas have consequences. Men can selflessly want to spread these ideas. Sometimes they may do this with some dispassion and sometimes they may do this in a messianic way. But not every popular book, magazine, or newspaper article was written " to make money." Not every motion picture or radio or television program was produced to control the thought of and to depersonalize someone else. They are often prepared to promote justice and to spread mercy. Crusading newspapers do not always become popular; they do not always gain in circulation. Yet they may enlarge crusades because they have a passion for civil justice, and it will not easily be downed. We can never understand the extent of the creative process unless we allow for a selfless promotion of ideas or structures of ideas (ideologies) through mass media.

Commerce. A second cluster of motivations for mass communication is the familiar and obvious economic motive. Most of the people who wish to promote unpopular ideas, creative visions, or improper opinions, have little access to mass media. Ordinarily, because of the enormous expense of production, they must content themselves with books of limited circulation or with "little magazines" and journals of opinion that gain their prestige by the quality of their presentation. Because of the expense of motion pictures and television, the profit motive has more nearly completely eliminated controversial subject matter.

In a free and competitive society the commercial motive does dominate in the spread of ideas and entertainment through mass media. Although governmental controls and ultimate popular reaction are minimal checks, the major responsibility falls to men who advertise over mass media or who must produce millions of copies of contacts for their effort to make it remuneratively worth-while. The impact of this situation on religion in a free society should be immediately apparent. An advertiser, for example, will seldom permit a religious television show that presents with any authority the exclusive claims of Protestantism, Roman Catholicism, Judaism, or secular religions (or antireligion!), because his program goes into the homes of potential customers who may react negatively. In religion and in other realms, such media as television have become notoriously safe. The churches, in their battles against programming offensive to themselves, have had to pay the price in uncontroversial, safe, and often insipid productions.

Control. Because of the pace, the extent, the pervasiveness, and the impact of mass media of communication, they have always been the targets and toys of men who would control other men. Biased communication, propaganda, irresponsibility, and demagoguery — all these have been frequent perversions of mass media.

We are familiar with the effective use to which Hitler, Mussolini, and the successive rulers of the U.S.S.R. have put radio as a means of extending totalitarian sway. We are familiar with the suppression of a free press and the rise of domesticated newspapers in the young dictatorships of Latin America. Big Brother of Orwell's nightmare *1984* knew well the effectiveness of mass media, and the brainwash can well occur through repetitions of propaganda and biased communication. These are, of course, extreme examples. All advertising, in a way, is an attempt at controlling the impulse of potential buyers. All persuasion verges toward the tendency to manipulate other people. Thus " idea or ideology," " commerce," and " control" tend to overlap. We are using them in a symbolic sense and thus making ideal types of them to illustrate throughout these pages the various reasons men communicate.

With these motives in mind we can easily see the reasons for the popularity of the media. First of all, response is hearty because the page or the program has been designed for consumption. Researchers into public opinion determine in advance what are the proper opinions for the seasons; they see how far an idea will go. They do research into human motivation: because of the economics involved, there is little room for experiment or adventure. So we might say that mass media are popular because they succeed in what they set out to do. They are not first of all designed to set standards and to lead man to some glorious paradise or brave new world. They are designed, to use one merchandiser's term, to give the lady what she wants. In it all, there is a quest for the least common denominator of public taste, which can be degraded a certain amount without controversy and can be raised somewhat without loss of audience. Still, there must be a certain stridency and shrillness in promotion, as typified by the tabloid headline. Minimal demands must be made on the intelligence or power of concentration — though here, again, there are exceptions. Sometimes a cluster of more profound psychological circumstances may help a *Doctor Zhivago* become a best seller or turn a "think piece" into a commercially profitable movie.

Another factor in the popularity of the media is their accessibility. They tend to come to us, through advertising, the mails, the turn of a knob. Without bestirring himself, a person can have the latest novel on the table because he belongs to a certain club. It is hard to resist magazine promoters. The neighborhood movie house made it difficult for the inner city legitimate stage. And radio and television invade kitchen and boudoir. Again, with careful calculation they appeal to many interests. Most Americans are interested in sports or stocks or race information or comics; in advertising, news, or editorializing. The newspaper presents them all in efficiently organized form. The offerings of all the media are particularly designed to cope with the boredom that is a mark of our leisure. Whoever has driven past the picture windows of a suburb on an autumn evening must wonder what people did before they had a picture tube into which to stare the hours away.

Sometimes underestimated is the way in which mass media curiously create kinship and community in an age when these are yearned for. "Have you read . . . ?" "Oh, I've seen that movie too." And instantly two women on a bus find a bond developing. There may be something extremely tangential, accidental, and temporary about such community. But any bond seems better than none.

A final element in the appeal of the media to which we may call attention is what might be termed their narcotic effect. Although it is possible to overdo the power of media such as television, they do also provide escape, alienation from the personal experiences that are too near; they are successful at numbing sensibilities and sensitivities. This is not necessarily a happy situation, but it does contribute to the popularity of the page and the program.

The complex of motives and reasons for popularity can be summarized in one sentence that immediately illustrates the effect on the Christian faith. Whether for ideology, commerce, or control, because of their design, simplification, and accessibility, and because of the escape and community they seem to create, the media, if they are truly *mass* media, set out to shape in men " the proper opinions," to make them common men and women, unknown citizens somehow at the mercy of the communicator. Because of the hours of attention they command and the apparent quality that is theirs owing to the economic potential, they usually achieve this aim. It is in such a world that Christianity makes its claim and its offer. It presents a paradox, a foolishness, something " contrary to the opinion." It has an Improper Opinion for the uncommon man, for the known citizen of the commonwealth whose builder and maker is God.

Chapter I

Forming Proper Opinions:
The Nonreligious Use of Mass Media

The communicator, in his interest in presenting ideas, selling products, or controlling persons, necessarily is involved in certain assumptions about man and society. There must be a common bond of discourse if there is to be any sort of communication with a person who does not understand the language, and it is virtually impossible to communicate any complicated ideas with precision through visual forms that abstract themselves from reality. There must be an understood language and understandable forms. There must be certain ground rules of discussion before the communicating game is begun.

Among these ground rules, whether they are made explicit or not, there will be certain assumptions about what man is, what honor and integrity are, what makes for propriety of opinion. Although, at the beginning, communicator and audience may not agree, they must at least speak the same language. The unconscious norm or setting for the presentation of opinion through mass media in our society is necessarily secular in nature. Any particular religious assumption, of course, would undercut the *mass* consumption that the communicator has in mind. Viewing communication in this light removes some of the opprobrium often cast by religious people on "secularist" producers of printed page or program. Now the producer appears merely as a reflector of society and not as a demonic distorter of religious values. Since we shall later make a point of the Christian's relationship, however indirect with this reflection, we must take some care to see what is involved in it.

Even the selection of the term for communication, which is neither generally religious nor specifically Christian, is difficult. In America communication via the printed page is rarely anti-Christian and almost never so in the programmatic media that do not permit selection to a skimming eye. To call it secularist implies that an articulate and self-conscious ideology is implicated. However, ordinarily the assumption is much more taken for granted than the suffix " ism " would suggest, and secular*ism* has become a bogey to many Christians. This only confuses things. We should say that the context is secular but not secularist, material but not materialist; it accurately depicts things as they are.

No word would better convey what we are after than " worldly " or " world-centered communication," though we shall have to desert that term too, because of its clutter. In this guarded context it can be enlarged upon. From the religious or Christian point of view, what does it mean that a society is secular or world-centered and that this characteristic is reflected in our public media?

" World " has first of all a symbolic value in Christian terminology. In its theological sense it does not apply at all to the created order, and indeed the Old Testament does not have the word. What was at first merely the totality of created reality (" all things," or " heaven and earth "), or specifically the human reality, changes in its theological setting. Because man is at the center of the world's meaning and because he is a rebel against God, his world is also seen to be in rebellion. Then " world " comes to mean " man in rebellion against God." When man closes his eyes against the vision of the light of God in order that he may pursue his own wisdom, he belongs to this world (II Cor. 1:22; Rom. 5:12; I John 2:17). What may normally be neutral — the things of the earth — become harmful when these things are surrogates for the grace and mercy of God in Christ Jesus. At times the world then is even granted a quasi-personal status, with a spirit of its own (I Cor. 2:12).

This world, then, which is essentially godless because of the rebellion, is the world that Jesus Christ saves after drawing upon himself its hatred. Those who are called by his name are frequently reminded that they are "not of this world," though they must live in the world. "Do not love the world or the things in the world." It is this symbolic sense of worldliness that was in the minds of moralists within the religious fold when they warned against certain books or magazines, certain motion pictures or television programs. Our society has been able to dull the sting of their judgments; but their instincts were theologically apt even when their strategies missed the mark. Presentation of our world with its basically secular cast, in forms that are dramatically vivid and pervasive, did and does present subtle threats to Christian proficiency.

If world, then, in this symbolic sense has a demonic cast, it also practically represents an opportunity or a potential to the Christian, in New Testament terms. The world is in rebellion but it is redeemable. The language seems archaic but the truth remains: although the "spirit" or the "prince" of the world may be past redemption, the world, when personalized, represents men and they can be rescued. This is a way of saying that for the Christian faith the decisive encounter of the Christian is with this world. He is to be wrapped up in its fears and hopes; its lineage and destiny are his own, and he cannot and should not escape them. The real battles are fought in this world. It is this world that God creates. In it he is incarnate in Jesus Christ. Here he dies, just as the rest of us do. And here the new creation breaks forth in the resurrection.

This leads many Christian thinkers to point to the potential character of creation and the persons who represent it. In this picture the sacred-secular antithesis must be overcome. The secular is potentially sacred. It bears in it the possibility of bearing also the Word of God who condescends to speak in the structures and realities of human life. Such a world is not the world of rebellion; it is the clay out of which God can make a new creation. We must keep this second understanding of the

world vividly before us if we want also to recognize later on
other possibilities of Christian relationship to the godless (but
possibly near-God) world.

In this world, which knows demonic ideas, demonic misuse
of people for commercial reasons, demonic power of control
over men, presentation of opinion in mass media today works.
The essential worldliness of the society must be exposed and
depicted, recognized and accepted, before any understanding
can come. If this necessity is kept in mind, we can ask, " What
did you expect? " when Christian hand-wringers complain of
the secularism of mass media and their patronizing attitude
toward Christian claims. We might even be grateful to the
media for their honesty at revealing to us a world as it is.
Through all the phoniness and illusion of the communicators'
worlds we learn again and again how time-and-space bound is
our present order. Christians owe the communicators a card of
thanks when this fact is allowed to shine through, stripped of
any religious or pseudoreligious pretensions.

The Christian who licks the stamp to apply to the card of
thanks is also conscious, however, that his own message and
life are immeasurably complicated by the nature of the world's
claim. This claim forms the ground rules, the understandable
language and symbol for communicator and audience. It is this
confluence of nearly ultimate secularization of the Western
world, with the ability to spread the basic ideas of that world
massively, that makes a crisis of mass communications for
Christians.

Here we must note how different matters would be were it
not for the confluence. Suppose mass media had been developed by the earlier, Christian West, or that the Christian character of the society still cast its weight in our day. In the light
of this picture, we see how impossible of recovery in the normal
course of history any significantly " Christian " view (in a particular sense) of mass media is. We are again, and foreseeably
we shall be, in the setting of the early Christians more than of

those who worked in the West (and often in the East) from the fourth to the seventeenth century.

The Christian society that existed from the Edict of Milan (a symbolic occasion) down to modern times would have assumed something entirely different of mass media. Then the ground rules, the understood language and accepted symbol, would have been those of Christendom or Christianity, or at least of religion. The City of God and the City of Man somehow overlapped each other. The spheres governed by God in his gospel, and by man with both his own and God's law, interacted with each other; they interpermeated each other and infused one another's value structures. What we would call church and state were somehow one, though jurisdictions may have been in dispute. In such an age Christianity, both in luxury and to its detriment, would have represented the setting for " the proper opinions " of the common man.

Picture what the Christian use of mass media would have meant in medieval times, if Père Congar's[3] description is accurate:

> The fact that (in principle) the church absorbed the world and imposed on it regulations proper to herself eventually meant the ignoring of the secularity of what is secular; preoccupation solely with the last end — the normal point of view of the clergy — led to the disregarding of secondary causes, the proper and immediate causes of things. . . . Medieval Christendom was, very generally speaking, a sacral regime, and by its hold of the spiritual over the temporal it brought about a union of the two that was in some ways premature and bought too cheaply. Earthly things were hardly considered except for their use in the church's sacred work, hardly at all in their own reality and causalities, and so they were not taken really seriously and received neither the attention they deserve nor the development they call for. . . . Only since the end of sacral Christendom, with its monastic and clerical setup, have we been able to get the full measure of the extent and requirements of the secularity of things and of the fidelity we owe them.

That paragraph illustrates the kind of society in which Christians could still have had complaint about nonreligious use of mass media and, in its last sentence, hints about the opportunities we shall describe in " the secularity of things " as reflected in the public media.

But the proper opinions of Christendom were negated and forgotten with the rise of the modern world. The world became again, after a millennium and a half, what it had always really been. After the medieval synthesis the air was cleared and the world was again seen to be not merely sacral but in rebellion and only potentially redeemable or sacred. It had come of age. It did not need the gods, or the God of the Christian faith. This coming of age occurred in every realm of the life that is now reflected by the communicators.

The fault, then, is not with authors and broadcasters, but with our times. If the mass media were suddenly to dedicate themselves to presenting " a Christian view of science," they would not even be understood by the bulk of their readers or hearers. For the world's assumptions are not those necessarily connected with religion or the Christian faith. The religious assumption that God represented the x in this year's equation was so frequently marred that eventually the scientist acknowledged that God had been edged out of the question itself. When this approach becomes the norm of the scientific community it would be arbitrary or deceitful were mass media to pretend that a different situation exists. We must, then, call the scientific assumption secular; but its secularity is not to be so obviously scorned.

A less controversial but even more obvious example would be the change in assumptions concerning the relation of church and state with the breakdown of Christendom and the rise of secularity. For most of the centuries from the fourth to the sixteenth, we have said, the mass communicator would only have had to report on the nature of the interpermeation or interpenetration of the two spheres of God's activity. But now most

Christians, particularly in America, accept a different view, which was historically of secular orientation, though credit for it is often claimed by Christians. We speak of " a wall of separation between church and state." Most politicians, statesmen, and commentators who employ the public media operate with the assumption that a separation of the realms of church and state, the spiritual and the secular order, is desirable. They assume, and this is accepted by churches in a pluralistic society, that no particular religion or religious emphasis should dominate or have a monopoly in the political order. We can only picture the disorder that would result were this worldly approach to be denied suddenly. Suppose that tomorrow the healthy secularity of mass media were forgotten and communicators proclaimed tenaciously and with fervor that all public offices should go to, say, Episcopalians; that glebe lands should be restored and that tithes and taxes should go to the support of this church; that thus God would again find his place in the lives of men. This would be unacceptable to over two hundred and fifty denominations in America. I even like to think that it would be unacceptable among Episcopalians.

The instance just offered points to one aspect of secularity that has been readily accepted by the churches, who saw no other practical course and who sometimes sought theological resources to make adjustments. But if in this instance nonreligious expression was desirable as a reflection of a nonreligious world situation, must one morally fault communicators when in other realms their world-centeredness dominates? They are only setting out to express what they are and what our times are, and Christians must start at other points (where desirable) to set them right.

It ought therefore to be no longer a surprise to find that secular assumptions, whether amoral or nonmoral, dominate the canons of art, entertainment, or education in mass media. These are parallel reflections of the centuries' long changes that we have cursorily chronicled. Into this changed world modern communications were born. They choose their norm, or it is imposed upon them, as if by the predestination that history works.

Now, I do not mean in this to propose that we must abandon the times or leave the world to its worldliness, the age-bound man to his telescoped vision. Not at all. But if the Christian is to find some bond with some indirect relationship to the world, he must first let it appear in its own light. He must let everything be what it is without trying to place a different light or color on it so that he may use it to his own purposes and for his own exploitation.

Nor must we suggest that world-centeredness or a nonreligious stance commits a communicator to selfish commerce or autocratic attempts at exercising power and control. The Christian must be ready to accept with enthusiasm and in a spirit of self-judgment the evidences of *justitia civilis*, a civil or human righteousness among those they would too readily write off as the children of darkness. When Mr. Pulitzer used to say that the function of his newspaper was to "afflict the comfortable and comfort the afflicted," he was dispensing justice and mercy within his own civil and secular framework in ways that should shame unthinking and apathetic Christians. All this should keep religious people from damning nonreligious efforts even where they may regret the changed assumptions of a "post-Christian" world.

Left to its own devices, however, the faults and failures of the nonreligious reflection of a nonreligious world become all too apparent. Even when religiously neutral, the public media tend to contribute to the depersonalization of man, which militates against Biblical conceptions of personhood. The man who uses these media to spread ideas or ideologies must seek the statistics of acceptance in the interest of efficiency. The man who dominates the air waves in the name of commerce is himself dominated by the degree of public acceptance: tyrannized by the economics of his presentation, he regards people not as persons but necessarily as objects. He must somehow remake them. The man who seeks to control others through the biased communication called propaganda cannot care for them as persons. They are things to be changed and used and ultimately subjugated. He does not begin by caring for their integrity or personhood.

So the media that possess such assets also carry with them their price. The routines and technical gains that make for efficiency and create primitive forms of community take their toll in values that Christians count to be important. This hazard becomes more and more apparent as we ascend the scale from the more deliberate, slower-paced, more static media toward the more dynamic, more restless, more ephemeral forms of contact.

The book still symbolizes the life of reflection. Even when we illustrate, pad, digest, or condense books, they require repeated and concentrated attention on the part of readers. In most books there is a certain amount of permitted waste in the matters of scene-setting, elaboration, or review. The reader is given opportunity to weigh and contrast, to appraise and absorb and reject. He keeps control in so many ways that the book can hardly be thought of with some of the other media as belonging to the mass: selectivity is at the heart of book choice and contact. Thus although the book may ultimately have the most profound impact of any of the forms of communication in question, it will ordinarily be appropriated critically. In times past when people still concentrated on *one* book, whether it was the Bible or Shakespeare or Gibbon, it was more likely to be *their* Bible or Shakespeare or Gibbon that was absorbed. They retained their critical faculties and had leisure to appropriate insights from reading into their organic view of the world.

When the pages of a book reflect the nonreligious character of our world, as do the works of Bertrand Russell or Jean-Paul Sartre or perhaps Ernest Hemingway, they create in the thoughtful person impressions that will outlast by decades those garnered from magazines or television programs. But the media that must make their impact in a matter of minutes so concentrate their assault on sensibilities that the recipient of the impact has less defense. The book, then, provides the best forum for reflection on the nonreligious character of our world but is least capable of subtly or insidiously undercutting values that the reader brings to the media.

With the magazine the pace is quickened to some extent. The writer or publisher assumes but momentary contact with a reader, who will soon reject the product for another magazine or the weekly or monthly successor of the one he holds. This means that there is less room for indirection or waste: now all energies must be collected toward a more sudden approach that will evoke immediate response, decision, and action. The normal magazine, with its advertising base, must count on the ability to prove that it influences people, as successful magazines regularly do. If action is to be achieved, this must occur while the magazine is current.

All this is even more true of the newspaper, which more readily yields to the temptation to use its reader. Particularly in metropolitan areas where thousands of newspapers are purchased on the basis of headline attraction, there is less likelihood that the civil dialogue can be sustained. The newspaper does provide opportunity for the crusader or the humanitarian who works with moral passion. But it must assume a certain popularity for the opinion the crusader would promote. He may champion a cause that is unpopular with an elite or a vested interest, but on a world-wide and permanent basis we cannot expect the unpopular opinion to make its way with the majority of readership. People may tolerate an eccentricity in a newspaper, e.g., spelling reform or a wayward columnist. But few newspapers have survived if they were too far out of step with the public. Thus the newspaper becomes a more effective means of rapid mass communication of ideas that lubricate the wheels of our society. In a more subtle and pervasive way it shapes the proper opinions that a majority of citizens feel to be necessary for consensus and common life.

As we progress through the media toward the more kinetic and dramatically potential we come next to the motion picture.

With accurate instinct, moralizers in the 1920's and 1930's reacted against the worldliness of this brawling and successful
medium. With similarly accurate instinct, producers of films
learned how to make a proper peace with the moralizers and
still to appeal to less than the highest instincts of a public they
sought less to transform than to reflect or cater to. A sensate
cultural era found satisfaction in a rather shoddy sensualism;
propagandists during the Second World War found the movies
to be the decisive medium for unifying a nation and building
hateful images of the enemy. When Clark Gable went without
an undershirt, the industry was seriously affected; when Mar-
lene Dietrich wore mannish slacks, all America did; when the
Japanese appeared as yellow devils, all the nation responded
with distaste and hatred.

The motion pictures were able to play this part in their heyday because they represented an interesting social phenomenon. They brought to the masses a form of entertainment once
accessible only to the cultured few. They reached into every
hamlet. The darkened movie theater provided an excellent setting for courtship. Production methods made possible a frequency of pictures that attracted people weekly (at least) at
modest prices. But despite all the energies that went into advertising and promotion, motion pictures did not mature as a
highly selective medium. Less frequently would people say,
" Let's wait and see such and such a movie " than they would
say, "It's Saturday and I'm bored; let's go down to the
Granada."

In such a setting, films that go against the stream or are
critical of society have a difficult time of it at the box office.
" Message " pictures or preaching films have rarely been impressively successful. Of all the media, the movies were the
most faithful reflectors of what society wanted or of what
direction it allowed itself to be led in. It was in this context
that I once heard the head of the Roman Catholic Legion of
Decency make sense of his agency's approach to movies. When
asked why Catholic magazines with an urbane audience often

were quite uncritical of moral ambiguities in Broadway plays
but so severe in moral condemnation of many movies, he explained: The energies, finances, and critical selectivity ex-
pended in investing in a set of tickets for two at a Broadway
play imply an informed and mature public. The Catholic conscience should be sufficiently refined to encounter the world
on these terms. But the casual, almost accidental exposure of
people of all ages and of most primitive conscience to the
readily accessible motion picture put a high premium on what
the church expects of it.

In these senses too the radio, which nearly saturates American sound waves in home and auto, bus and supermarket, is ordinarily a reflector of its society that makes its way more quietly
and insidiously into the value patterns of its listeners than do
the media that are selected by critical people. Television is a
nearly ultimate example of this need and possibility to form the
proper opinions in masses of people. Within the space of minutes the viewer must be convinced of certain ideas, products,
or actions. He can be conscientiously polled, used, calculated.
His chances for selectivity are not nearly so wide as they were
with books or magazines; he may turn a dial to eliminate one
Western only to find three or four others interchangeable with
it. The expense of production and broadcasting and the varieties of eyes and ears the medium encounters make necessary
an appeal to popularity that is seldom transcended. Rather
grudgingly, religious or intellectual programs are given a place,
but never at " prime time " — instead usually in the Sunday
morning religious blackout ("when the saints are in church
and the sinners in bed ") or the Sunday afternoon intellectual
ghetto (when people with sense are out in the park or on the
beach).

In summary we might say that the more kinetic and nonselective a medium is and the more expensive its production,
the more necessary it is that a massive audience be assembled.
This audience will permit itself to be challenged or stirred only
within a very limited context. A secularized world will reflect

itself ordinarily in quite a frontal way to an uncritical nation. The dangers to the Christian faith are readily apparent here.

Such dangers will seldom take the form of *anti*religious uses of the media. Religion is so safely and comfortably embedded in the nation's mores that it provides a protective shield also around Christianity. Attacks therefore would run counter to popular and proper opinions and are not likely to occur. However, the more static and selective media may have some room for criticism of religion. There are occasional books of sizable circulation that attack religion and the Christian faith. But film makers have learned to be very cautious in criticism, and an antireligious television broadcast is almost unthinkable in America's cultural context. Far more frequently is the Christian faith undercut when its option is not taken seriously, when it is neglected and dismissed, not as being untrue or dangerous, but as being unimportant.

On other levels the presentation of a nonreligious world to a world that still has room for some religion and for some Christian people complicates Christian response. The obvious example was cited in the reference to the Legion of Decency and the movies. Nonreligious communication in mass media may, and perhaps ordinarily will, reflect not the best in the modern world: a high humanism and an impassioned social concern that challenges men as men. More likely it will appeal to the less noble instincts. The sensual appeal of films and television (and, of course, best-selling books) has been notorious. The appeal is normally made in a proper and respectable manner; for this reason, it has served even more to undercut not only puritanism but also the healthy safeguards Christianity has built up against depersonalizing sex for self-gratification.

People who would, in the name of respectability, avoid a controversial foreign film of earthy reputation, which does anything but glamorize sexual relationships, will regularly by osmosis be absorbing a set of sensual values that present greater difficulties to Christian concentration and discipline. It would not be easy to picture someone becoming casual about the

Seventh Commandment or the Sermon on the Mount's strictures against lust after viewing postwar Italian "neorealist" movies. In these, sexual relationships were presented more frankly than they are in most domestic films. But the sordidness, the ennui, and the terror of the lost lives of their heroes and heroines would do anything but attract. The technicolored cinemascopic concentration on anatomical detail that characterizes most acceptable American films is a far more attractive invitation to depart from Christian standards of morality.

Lest this illustration be too drawn out on an obvious matter (and lest we be written off as tired puritans), we could illustrate other ways in which the self-presentation of a nonreligious world — at its worst — can characterize mass media. The commercial standard there typified is subversive of Biblical concepts of stewardship. The "American Way of Life" as there depicted is incompatible with Christian canons of sacrifice and service. The political or ideological attempt to control others violates Christian interest in personhood and integrity. The concentration on the merely diverting or the trivial dulls the imagination and stifles creative energy.

None of these perversions *need* occur in the use of mass media; that they normally do occur needs little documentation. Whatever the age's ills, they are likely to be reflected, albeit somewhat glossily, in the mass media. There is, understandably, no theonomous reference, no "vertical" responsibility to God. The over-all effect is one of trivialization or benumbing. This effect will tend to increase as the pervasiveness and relative instantaneousness of the media spread. Fundamentalist colleges that do not permit students to see movies of the highest quality in theaters seldom have rules against viewing banal " C " pictures over television. Cartoonists relish the intrusion television makes on the way of life of monks in their cloisters. If these are trivial instances, we know they can be amplified in more serious directions in the fields of justice, economics, race, personal conduct. Mass media are dangerous because they have no standard of judgment higher than that which belongs to the age, to people in collectives (who erode one another's stand-ards or cancel them out). They present, then, an illusion of ac-ceptability and propriety. Habit-forming, they can dull judg-ment. All this can happen. Later, we want to show that this need not be the *only* form of presentation of the nonreligious world in these media and that Christians have a stake in im-proving them also at the secular level.

For now it is enough to say that the normal activity of mass media is to convey the kind of value or opinion that is gen-erated by a thoroughly secularized society with a religious veneer. The first task of the Christian church is to be vigilant; to assist in interpreting this nonreligious world; to engage in thoughtful criticism of the dehumanization of this world. Con-sistently we must remind ourselves that no approach to the mission of the church today makes sense if it assumes that any substantial number of people can resist the influences of the mass media that broadcast in print or sound or image the gen-erative impulses of their society. We cannot keep them from people and we cannot keep people from them. We cannot realistically expect to " convert " the whole society and thus the media, and we cannot faithfully suggest surrender. Other ways must be found to confront the nameless citizen of a ma-ture world with the paradox of Christianity.

Chapter II

Forming Proper Opinions:
The Religious Use of Mass Media

Nonreligious publication, production, or broadcast of ideas and images is not too difficult to unmask. Whether the approach is frontal and patent or whether it is quiet and implicit, the reflection of secularity in mass media can be recognized by the informed Christian. He can see that it either undercuts or at least complicates his sense of mission.

Not so with religious use of mass media. In a world that no longer finds God to be a necessary option, it is somehow comforting to hear people talk about God to great masses. In a world in which churchgoing is neglected over huge geographical areas, it is somehow reassuring to be told by advertisers to attend the church or synagogue of one's choice, to help children find a faith. In a world in which reverence is cheap if not disappearing, it often seems as if the Christian church has found allies among those who in best seller or benediction would "teach us to pray." In an impious world, every trace of piety, it would seem, should be regarded as an ancilla, a handmaiden to the worship of God.

When man is defiant and hate builds walls; when warfare and weapons are the order of the day; when people are uncertain and in quest of security; when the alternatives seem to be confusion and apathy and chaos — in such a world and such a time, he would certainly seem an ingrate who looks twice at any religious use of mass media. I intend to show that, in America at least, the greater threat to the Christian faith

48

today in the matter of the communications field is not from the camp of the secularist but from the religionist.

When we speak of religion in this sense, it is obvious that we are dealing with a sticky category. A dramatic definition of the term is certainly meant, for often in Christendom religion and the Christian faith are equated. Indeed, for us, they have many relations and harmonies. It will therefore be necessary for us to take some pains to show in what ways religion, in a secularized world, does the faith a disservice.

Religion here involves a complex of definitions. Most frequently in a religiously pluralistic society that sanctions religion, it must involve the attitudes of reverence toward an ill-defined object. It implies an interest in a nameless, faceless god. It concerns itself more with the religious subject than with the religious object; it is fascinated with the response of man more than with the possible initiative of gods. However strong its Christian reminiscence in our society, religion in this broadcast sense is largely devoid of content; it is creedless and aimless. Ordinarily it implies a pious stance and bearing, a certain personality type, perhaps even a certain metaphysic that needs "God" in place of the x in equations.

Such religion in such a society must be inoffensive to any minority. It must describe God in terms sufficiently broad to be universally respectable. It must describe piety as "the thing to do." When seen in the context of Biblical faith, such religion does a disservice in that it provides man with insulation against the surprising interruption of God in Christ. Generalized religion in this sense belongs to the alien powers described in the New Testament. It assumes that there is something beyond man that controls his life or that can be controlled by man; but the clarity of Biblical religion is necessarily denied.

A man's religious life imprisons him against Christ. His religiousness, far from causing him to be open, makes him on the contrary as if obsessed. His ears are stopped to the message of Christ. Mohammedans are just as incapable even of grasping the idea of becoming Christians, thus harkening to the message of an earlier time, as we Christians are of imagining that we should become Jews, since for us Israel's religion represents a preliminary stage. It is exactly the same with other religions. The more religious a man is, the less prepared he is to hear.[4]

We have no difficulty in seeing this condition in a world environment. The well-known resurgence of the world religions — Islam, Hinduism, Buddhism, Shinto — occurring in the middle of the twentieth century has infinitely complicated the Christian mission in our time. Entirely apart from the fact that Christianity is often associated with Western aggression and with dreams in the world of rising nationalism and anticolonialism, we have all been made aware of the difficulty religions as religions have presented to Christian evangelists. This is in marked contrast to the successes of Christians in their work a century ago, when they often found it possible to pour their proclamation into a relative spiritual vacuum. It is not difficult to agree, then, that the better a Mohammedan or Buddhist a man may be, the more difficult would it be to present the Christian faith to him.

We can even see evidences in the West of the ways religions provide insulation and protection against God's interruption of man's history in Jesus Christ. This is particularly true in those places in the West ("Christendom") where secularity has matured into new religions. What was nazism but the absolutizing of a secular way of life that found ready metaphysical and pseudohistorical sanction and symbolic and ceremonial undergirding? Now we are coming closer to home: in Germany, during the rise of the terror, there were *Deutsche Christen*, German Christians, who found it possible to take religious elements of Christian culture and its *mythos* and render them serviceable to an ideology and power thrust that manifestly contradicted the Christian good news. To a lesser degree this Christian overlay and heretical intrusion has been seen here and there where communism had to make its way in a previously Christian world. When an ideology hardens into a religion, bearing an approach to ultimacy, the faith is guarded against even where coercion does not prevent its intrusion.

Another step closer: in Western " Free " Europe, Americans are wont to see a secularization they deny in their own milieu. The obvious standards of religious revival and success are missing: church attendance is not high. The intellectuals have little use for Christian claims. Voluntary financial support of Christian causes is negligible. The world has matured and no longer finds the religion of Christian reminiscence tenable or attractive. In such a culture two types of people are most difficult to approach in the name of Jesus Christ. One is the man who has plunged himself into the world in a hedonistic way, making a religion of his ultimate attachment to pleasures of sense. " The more religious a man is " about such a view, the less prepared he is to hear. The other is the intellectual, who has sophisticated his involvement in " the existential " or " the absurd " or even " the nation " to the point that it becomes a religious attachment. He, too, does not often hear.

If this happens in what frequently seems to Americans to be the dry tree, something similar also occurs in the green. There where, as they see it, life holds fresh promise, where " the juice is running," religion has its way: how can this religion stand in the way of the Christian faith? But soon, on closer examination, we can see that timeless temptations have merely found new dress in the religions that make up what is euphemistically known as " the American Way of Life." Our first clue to the doctrinal consistency of this Way (however diffuse and ill-defined the dogmas) comes from the uniqueness of the term. Something entirely different would be implied if we talked about the Korean way of life, or the Swiss or Monacan or even Cuban way of life. Then only a set of economic or social patterns is considered. The American Way of Life is enhanced by ideological sanctions and ceremonial lip service. Americanism can be such a sanction or religion; un-Americanism is its antichrist. We cannot even picture " un-Puerto-Ricanism " or " un-Scotlandism "!

Our refusal to recognize this tendency toward making a re-

ligion of what should remain proximate values was clear from
the frantic response of Americans to Karl Barth's repeated (and
admittedly somewhat naïve) defenses of the world behind the
Iron Curtain. In order to make a dramatic point about the
absolutisms of our selfish system he was forced into depicting
in unnaturally roseate hues the virtues of the Soviet system,
which Americans unitedly abhor. Our reaction, however, obscured the value in his prophecy: that whether we uphold it in
apathy or in tenacity, the American Way is capable of being
another barrier to hearing the Word of God.

Once we admit this possibility, we must see how the many
good things which reinforce that way and that life have a
double-sidedness which, when seen not under judgment, work
against Christianity. Whenever man insulates himself, through
propriety and assumptions about native goodness, from the
judgment and grace of God, he is in the Christian point of view
erecting idols and altars that keep him from Jesus Christ. These
are not uniquely American vices, but our national successes
and prosperity have made them national temptations in a
uniquely high degree. It may be a do-it-yourself cult or a new
status; it may be a service club or lodge or church with an
" onward and upward " bent; it may be a surrender to the
suburban dream and a denial of human need in our tech-
nologically manufactured paradise — whatever it is, our attachment to these Pelagian outlets keeps us from hearing, and as
religions they do us disservice. The fact that we make such
provision for defending this way of life to the background of
organ tones and the glow of stained glass contributes to the
image that a secularized world has of America. We are self-
conscious, bustling, adolescent. We will outgrow this. We will
come of age.

All these impulses form the background in which Christianity and Judaism are presented in the attempt to form proper
opinions over mass media. It would be entirely beside the point
to suggest that such formation is always due to bad motives;
indeed, criticism of religious use of mass media is so complex

and suspect because it seems to cast shadows of suspicion on children of light come to help us. If they seem to have a zeal for God, even if it is not according to knowledge, should they not be acknowledged? We may admire and thank them as persons; that does not relieve Christians of the responsibility of critically evaluating their well-meant endeavors. Again, we can profitably assess these motives and achievements under the categories of ideology, commerce, and control.

First of all, there are good ideological reasons for presenting the general religiousness that characterizes the American Way through mass media of communication. The best reason is the simplest: men believe in it and they want to share this evangel. The American Way of Life has not commended itself easily as a missionary faith. Its preconditions of geography, natural resources, heritage, and citizenship make it in many ways the exclusive property of those born to share it. Still, elements in its credo of good will have made it what its best theologian called it, " the last, best hope of earth." There is a certain contagion to this vision which even foreign visitors often accept after excusing us for the excesses caused by our adolescence as a spiritual entity. The enthusiasm caused by participating in an earthly paradise, with its benefits full, pressed down, and running over, prompts men to promulgate such views en masse. A second good reason for ideological support of American religiousness is the way it can help sustain a national consensus, can be a glue for common purposes.

By this we mean that the American kind of national religion that embraces the particular faiths has, from the time of the founding fathers down to our day, been a fortunate undergirding of national resource. From the first we were destined to be a pluralistic society with coexisting and competing faiths. Happily, the competition has seldom been bloody or even personally damaging. This was true in part because of the resources of Biblical faith that proved to be forthright but not intolerant. Another contributing spirit was the tolerant character of the Enlightened age when the nation was born. If these assets were put to test as a variety of Protestant groups made their way to American shores, if they were strained as Roman Catholicism became statistically strong and articulate and as Judaism and even non-Biblical faiths acquired fair representation, we must say that the religiousness of Americans, committed or uncommitted to the historic faiths, has been a sign of health. Here is a value we would wish to see preserved even in a time when assertion of particularity is valid and valuable. This is why interpretation rather than extinction of religious as well as nonreligious ideologies of a durable character represents a more realistic strategy for American Christians.

So, because men believe in God, in brotherhood, in a common way of life and because they desire to keep that way of life, they will continue to present it with religious overtones. The mass media of communication have provided a salutary and certainly necessary means of fostering the way. When men lived in isolation from one another — Congregationalists in New England, Anglicans in Virginia, Presbyterians in Kentucky, Lutherans in Minnesota, Roman Catholics in New Orleans — mutual understanding was a luxury. As diagrammatic views of American life broke down and a new interpersonal jostling came about in this mobile and nomadic nation, understanding became a necessity. If God, the flag, " eternal values," mother, church, and the dollar sign were somehow wrapped up with each other in pious support of a heritage, who would criticize this, top to bottom?

Of course, criticism seems necessary when this religious pattern appears in direct contradiction of Christian claims. From time to time American religion has had prophets who might be called explicitists. They want to take the intuitive and inherited wisdom of a people, the pragmatic way Americans have of solving problems in a democratic process, and harden it into a dogmatic religion that would obscure the validity of particular faiths. Such syncretism seems to appear somewhere in every nation's life and has appeared in America particularly when its pluralism seemed to render it impotent against foreign idea patterns. Such an ideology has had to be resisted in the name of the God of the Christian faith. Needless to say, the explicitists are outnumbered by those who quietly accept the assumptions of pragmatic, generalized, and creedless religion.

Because overarching religious appeals are inoffensive and yet satisfy religious longings, however illusory the satisfactions may be, they are attractive to communicators. This leads us to the second cluster of reasons for religious use of mass media — the commercial. When uncertainties about our way of life are soothed by religion, when anxieties about our place in the scheme of things internationally (and in outer space) plague us, we turn for reassurance to the unctuous pacifiers with their gospels of peace of mind and peace of soul. It is significant that during the 1950's scarcely a single work of specifically scientific character reached best-seller status. This was true despite the fact that the scientist was often regarded, as Robert Fitch likes to say, as "priest and savior," with a sort of religious awe. It was true even though the race for space was on many lips and though science fiction had a large and cultic following.

But the best-seller lists of books included titles like *Peace of Mind, Peace of Soul, Peace with God, The Power of Positive Thinking*. Mass somnolence and comfort were offered with astonishing similarity by men of varying religious visions. The response suggested the commercial validity of the effort to present religion in these terms, however questionable the nature of the presentation in the light of Biblical faith, which is geared to the failures and the offscourings of the world. Some numinous sense has nurtured Americans even in a time when Western man characteristically describes himself as godless. Somehow these longings must be satisfied, and they can be satisfied most profitably in terms of least common denomination and most common inclusion. Elements in Judaism that offended Christians were obscured by Joshua Loth Liebman; his Christian counterparts could even talk about the cross and the resurrection and somehow make it something less than the scandal, the improper opinion on which Christian life is nurtured after it is quickened.

Within this commercial context, the particular faiths that represent significant minorities — say, from one to forty million people — could be presented over mass media without offense if they were tailored for this purpose. By itself, each of these options: Judaism, Zen, the world religions, Protestantism, Catholicism, could make its way in mass presentation so long as it would not be disruptive of the American way of life. Rarely would a sponsor, however, associate himself with a national broadcast that promoted a particular faith (commercial television sponsorship of some time for Bishop Sheen is an exception) because the demand for " equal time " by other purchasers of the same toothpaste or detergent would be embarrassing to the communicator who for commercial reasons must make an inclusive appeal.

So instead of presentations of the historic faiths, the religious communication of which we here speak usually came under one of two headings. It might promote what John Dewey called " a common faith." " After all, we are simply taking different boats to the same shore." " After all, it doesn't make any difference what you believe so long as you believe." " After all, so long as you're a good American and believe in God it doesn't make much difference what you call yourself." Criticism of this common faith from the viewpoint of Christianity should scarcely be necessary. However, Christians are in the habit of performing delicate if automatic acts of translation when they read or hear such versions of religion. Against a Christian reminiscence and in the setting of a once-Protestant environment, they are inclined to fill in the outlines, to draw lines to connect the dots, whenever religion is mentioned. We are all for it.

The second conventional way of presenting religion or religions is actually much fairer, though it is distinctly in the minority because of the delicate task of being fair. This is a method which is conscious of pluralism and is desirous of pro-

moting the American consensus by informing people about the
particular faiths that generated the healthy coexistence we
have known. In this approach, the particular faiths are presented as options. If *The Saturday Evening Post* includes Paul
Tillich in its series on "Adventures of the Mind," sooner or
later it will include François Mauriac. *Harper's* would not
think of presenting the case for Judaism without giving spokes-
men for Protestantism, Catholicism, and — in one rare instance — agnosticism an opportunity. After a number of portrayals of priests in motion pictures, there is sure to be also a
Protestant "Man Called Peter." Christmas television finds it
necessary to enlarge the Jewish Feast of Hanukkah out of all
historic significance because inevitably traces of Christian culture will appear over the commercial medium in ways that will
seem unjust or partial and thus also damaging to advertising
promotions. Round tables and forums and symposia have been
effective ways of dealing with this delicate problem to commercial satisfaction. Place a rabbi, a priest, and a minister, distinc-
tively garbed, around a coffee-laden table and let them talk.
Incidentally, this approach does provide for most articulate
presentation of particular faiths in settings of highest personal
congeniality and thus of highest potential hope.

We need not comment in detail on the political or social uses
of religion that serve to control or manipulate others. Sometimes this occurs in the name of Christian evangelism when
rhetoric, crowd-appeal, the sense of this being "the thing to
do," force people to what is called voluntary, but is unthinking,
response. More often it occurs in hours of national crisis (one
thinks of McCarthyism) when a flag with a cross serves to induce panicky people to confuse national ideal with religious
purpose. Our pluralistic society fortunately makes this possibility the least likely motive for religious use of mass media at
present. Those last two words point to the necessity, however,
of being ever vigilant.

If religious use of television, radio, the printed page, means
first of all the opportunity to present inclusive, diffuse, and non-

controversial religion, we can go farther. We might say that
because of the deposit of Christianity in the structures of Western society, there is room to speak of religion as a *praeparatio
evangelica*, a precondition for the Christian faith. Just as
Christianity made its way by encountering, interpreting, and
transforming the religion of the Old Testament and later
Judaism, and just as missionaries from time to time have
adapted themselves to native culture, so American Christians
can take the societal, utilitarian residue of Christendom that
remains in a not yet totally secularized culture and build on
from there.

This has been tried; one form of apologetics permits the use
of existing religion as it is fused with culture for the building up
of the Christian faith. The Acts of the Apostles (ch. 17) includes a speech that it says Paul delivered at Athens. This was
there his approach:

"I perceive that in every way you are very religious. ... What
therefore you worship as unknown, this I proclaim to you. ...
And [God] made from one every nation of men to live on all
the face of the earth, having determined allotted periods and
the boundaries of their habitation, that they should seek God,
in the hope that they might feel after him and find him. Yet he
is not far from each one of us, for ' In him we live and move and
have our being '; as even some of your poets have said, ' For we
are indeed his offspring.' ... The times of ignorance God over-
looked, but now he commands all men everywhere to repent,
because he has fixed a day on which he will judge the world in
righteousness by a man whom he has appointed, and of this
he has given assurance to all men by raising him from the
dead."

Most of the religion of this passage falls under the "proper
opinion " rubric. Sooner or later, though, even the religious
Paul had to become the Christian Paul, and at the mention of
the improper opinion, the scandal of the Christian faith, he lost
his audience. The editor of the speech and the author of the
narrative seem to be singularly halfhearted about the half-

hearted response given it. Paul does not seem to try the approach so directly again. Yet there is some warrant for the attempt on the part of those who know what they are doing.

The dangers are manifest. One can, with John Baillie,[5] sophisticate this form of apology and speak of "the other who is most near" in Western society. This civilization's art and institutions have a Christian afterglow on which one can build. The sign of the cross is virtually omnipresent. Whatever problems this raises for Christianity in its world-wide mission, the fact strikes me as being the most promising apologetic for domestic consumption. But it has its hazards: it first of all appeals in a constantly more secularized world to a residue that is constantly more easily dismissed. The Christianity of Christendom had its place under the sun and has been displaced. It was tried and found wanting. Vital Christianity today makes its approach on different grounds. Such an approach is not only hazardous, it becomes more difficult to try year by year as the signs of Christian influence in a particular sense are swallowed up, absorbed, or corroded.

Another way to use the Christian religion to promote the Christian faith occurs in the kind of apologetic we associate with names like C. S. Lewis. Again, as with that of Dr. Baillie, it is a form I find congenial, and as a Christian I am fascinated, if not spellbound, by it. But ultimately I must say that it too can do no more than clear away debris so that the only scandal associated with the Christian faith is the one proper to it. Often I would have to agree with Lewis' detractors that the effort represents a sleight of hand, particularly in the hands of lesser figures. If one grants too much in the premises to an opponent, it is difficult to win the point of particularity. Thus it was as long ago as the second century, when apologists attempted to build on by adding the concept of the seminal logos. Thus it was when liberal Christianity placed its message on the escalator of evolution or the continuum of natural progress. Either particularity of Christianity is potentially absorbed by the more inclusive affirmation, or there comes that moment when the sleight of hand is gone, when one is no longer all things to all men: " Now when they heard of the resurrection of the dead, some mocked; but others said, ' We will hear you again about this ' " (Acts 17:32). So there is always danger and always hope. Here it is necessary to point out that when Christendom or a Christian heritage is used as the groundwork for the Christian faith, as a precondition or an a priori, the communicator must always be aware that the casual reader or listener is all along translating this to terms that will make Christian claims later untenable.

If a generalized religion can be presented for ideological or commercial reasons, or as a means of manipulating people; and if the Christian religion can be presented as a precondition for the Christian faith, there is a third way of presenting Christianity as a religion that apparently offers even more than the preconditioning (and at least partly laudable) way.

This third way is little more than an extension into the world of mass media of the method of presenting the Christian faith of which all within the Christian community would approve. We speak of formal, direct, explicit witness to the activity of God in Jesus Christ. If, however, we examine this method in its extended form, we shall see a curious transformation taking place: in the mass market place it too tends to take on the trappings of what we are here calling religion. It can employ mass media *in relation to the Christian community* and achieve the desired effect. The shut-in, the irregular churchgoer, the regular worshiper involved in acts of supererogation, all these can benefit from inclusion in the sometimes ersatz and always marginal sense of community that mass media can bring. It is thus possible to eavesdrop on Christian worship with some benefit, as is done when Christmas Midnight Mass is telecast or when the more progressive churches radio-broadcast their services. It is possible for the already committed to become more committed by the respectability that mass presentation of the Christian faith can bring, by the increase in knowledge or inspiration it can provide. These are assets when Christians know precisely what is happening. They are liabilities when they create an illusion about success and response, or when Christianity is watered down for mass consumption, or when it does the faith a disservice by making its explicit claim vulnerable to easy dismissal by the nonreligious world. These dangers are more imminent in the use of less selective, more pervasive and kinetic media than in reasoned discourse on printed page.

We are now at a difficult phase of the argument, and some illustration is in order. In the matter of books, the least vulnerable field, best-selling presentations of faith either offer what Christianity does not itself promise (*Peace with* . . .), or they fasten on the merely fascinating or curious elements (as in Jim Bishop's *The Day Christ Died*), or they attract a large enough audience within " the mass " of the already committed that they do not even become part of the market place of ideas (one thinks of Billy Graham's explicit *Peace with God* in paperback form). Again, let it be said that books provide excellent opportunities for presentation of the Christian faith on particular, profound, and winning terms, because books appeal to a select audience within a mass. One buys a book; he does not dismiss it as easily as he turns a dial.

That the dangers exist in the field of periodical literature was made clear in an article by Robert Ostermann, editor of *The Voice of St. Jude,* in *The Writer's Digest* (October, 1959, pp. 19 ff.). Mr. Ostermann, in presenting " Ten Commandments for Religious Writers," was himself partly guilty of turning over Christian and religious possibilities to too-neat packagers (e.g., "IX: Try a Little Controversy " — notice, do not try a big controversy!) His Fourth Commandment, "Do Not Preach," makes sense:

> Every successful new writer can be damned by one temptation should he succumb to it. God help him if he feels he must preach. At least eight out of ten writers who knock at my door are frustrated preachers. They must tell readers what to do: they want to prescribe and legislate; they must be conclusive. They have a message and they would not dream of delivering

it indirectly; they insist on being as clear and dogmatic as the pope. Preaching always gives answers. Some of us think that most readers do not even know what the questions are and we are not afraid of a reader's having an idea of his own.

The magazine has become an excellent forum or hostel for symposia in which several religious options are offered; as such, even the truly mass-circulation journals present hope.

The newspaper is another problem. Because contact must be instantaneous and response immediate, the temptations grow. Here the explicit presentation of Christianity degenerates into religion, as in the famous series of advertisements by the Knights of Columbus in which the Catholic religion was presented with sleight-of-hand techniques; or it is easily dismissed — witness the disregard with which explicit advertisements for Sunday sermons are passed by readers (including Christians) of the Saturday papers. We shall have more to say later concerning the more profitable ways for Christianity to present itself in the metropolitan press.

In motion pictures the necessarily noncontroversial character of the medium from the religious point of view makes it necessary to show Christianity in most cases as an easily dismissible (or absorbent) reality. The clergyman-hero is ordinarily a "nice" but harmless person; his message is either devoid of content or curious. Exceptions are few. The investor in a motion picture for the secular market can scarcely be blamed if he favors no religion unless it numbers thirty or forty million people and unless his presentation seriously offends no one else.

Radio has become the most convenient forum for explicit presentation of the Christian religion. "Come to Jesus" appeals are plentiful on Sunday broadcasts, where — because the message is presented out of the context of communal worship — the tendency is toward highly individualistic religion. "Accept Jesus Christ as your *personal* Savior" is the characteristic manner. This has an appeal to those committed, and performs a useful if highly restricted function among them. Radio provides an economical way to overhear communal worship, which is certainly an attractive possibility to the sick and shut-in minority. It provides an excellent opportunity for presenting the didactic or nutritive side of Christianity, though it has seldom been used for it. Usually it distorts the Christian message into a promise-all and demand-nothing version of cheap grace or expensive moralism, or its explicitness is so ill-mannered or private that it encourages dial-twisting. I have often thought, while driving an auto on a Sunday evening in "Protestant" areas, that were I not a Christian, most religious radio would keep me from being or becoming one. Radio is just economical enough to permit broad access to communicators, just inclusive enough to be considered a mass medium, even if only regionally.

Television, because of costs, has been more restrictive; religious broadcasting on it tends only to be uncreative and to reflect some of the low morals that its normal time spots, far from "prime time," induce. Explicit presentation of the Christian faith out of cultural context probably occurs less on television than in any other medium except the motion picture. The implicit possibilities, we shall see in a later chapter, are manifold.

So many of the efforts to expose the Christian faith to masses of people come under the category "the harm that good men do." There is no question but that they have a popular appeal to Christian supporters. I have seen men in the fields of religious radio and television almost embarrassed at the financial support they receive from the laymen who determine denominational budgets. There is something glamorous, current if not avant-garde, something progressive and — perish the thought! — *efficient* about spreading the Christian gospel broadcast by press and over air waves or through film. Fundamentalist groups in particular have seen the possibilities of establishing their integrity by presenting the old-time religion in this new-time manner. Often their efforts have been well-meaning and to the degree that they have borne fruit in the Christian world they do not come under scrutiny here.

But to the degree that in the secular world religious use of mass media builds barriers to the Christian faith or against it, to that degree, serious revision is in order. When it waters down the Christian faith for mass consumption, it contributes to making it a religion, a proper opinion of use to ideologist, advertiser, and demagogue. When it is explicit in the wrong context, its form of apology makes quieter Christian work more difficult. By our dramatic definition, religion is not a fruitful category for Christian approach in the employment of mass media of communication.

Chapter III

Forming the Improper Opinion:
The Christian Use of Mass Media

The normal and efficient use of the communications media aims
to promote the kind of opinions that can be held by masses of
men. In the interest of promoting ideas or ideology, the communicator is desirous of " selling a thought " that is sufficiently
inoffensive that a majority of his audience or readership will
buy it. In the interests of commerce, the advertiser concerns
himself with avoiding scandal, being safe, and tailoring his
product and its claims to the widest possible market. In the
interest of controlling masses of people with a political idea,
the propagandist or biased communicator will through a variety of arts seek to bring the people under his sway.

We have tried to establish that this normal use of mass media
raises few problems for nonreligious communication. Such use
need be nothing more than a reflection of what the culture or
society already really is. Although there is room for a critical
and prophetic note or for some anticipation and pace-setting,
these must be inserted in a context of the immediately realizable
or acceptable, else the communication does not long belong to
the mass. It is interesting to note that journals which go somehow against the grain of society assume a smaller readership
from the outset and are called " journals of opinion." *The Nation, The New Republic, The Commonweal,* for example, live
with limited circulation hopes. If they wanted to move from
the thirty to fifty thousand subscriber circle to the one million
readership mark, they know this increase could not be brought

about merely by improvements in their advertising or marketing or in the quality of their production. It could come only if
they decide to gain the whole world and lose their own souls
or lives. *The Saturday Evening Post* and *Life* magazine do indeed have opinions. These may be subtly expressed but they
are consistent and formative. Yet they are opinions that through
the test of the years are probably on the side of acceptability
and propriety.

Just as in nonreligious publishing, production, and broadcasting, so, we have tried to suggest, pluralistic America has de-
vised ingenious ways of promoting religious use of mass media
in the context of propriety of opinion. " The Religion in American Life " program is an enduring illustration of this phenomenon. Through its relation with an advertising council, R.I.A.L.
is able to secure a great amount of space on billboards, in magazines, and on television. A well-meant attempt, it must stress
the wholly acceptable features of the spiritual life. Either the
worshipers it portrays are pictured in a contrivedly nonde-
nominational setting or, in the background, three buildings will
be suggested: a basilican type of structure for Roman Catholicism, a synagogue for Jews, a colonial structure for Protestantism. The very nature of R.I.A.L.'s campaign, designed simply to promote churchgoing and to foster the idea that faith is
useful to families and in society, would be subverted were any
particular or offensive elements introduced. This is not said in
criticism of such programs, but rather in interpretation and to
suggest their limitations.

The difficulty for Christians in their use of the mass media
of communication is this: even the simplest reduction of the
Christian faith transgresses the ground rules of both nonreligious and religious presentations. Although there is an admirably rich deposit of Christianity that is broadly acceptable
to humanity, the heart of the faith is not. The products of the
faith — the works of love, the human spirit, the life of service
— are the gifts of the faith in its better moments to all men in

society. But the generative impulse of these products — response to the demand of God and to his loving call in Jesus Christ — represents a departure from the broadly acceptable and proper.

We are prepared, then, to face some of the implications of the scandal of Christian particularity and the impropriety of its basic opinion. This forces us to introduce a term which has perhaps been overused in recent Christian theological discourse and which has many technical shadings that we do not care to call into discussion here. The word is "paradox"; as we examine its rootage and its intention and clarify some misconceptions concerning it, we can see its place in the discussion of opinions.

The term came into new respectability (propriety?) in twentieth-century theology partly in reaction against the wholly liberal reduction of the faith. The tendency to place Christian revelation in a continuum that was exhausted by the natural order matured during the nineteenth century. The critical tradition called into question the uniqueness of God's revelation in his Word, Jesus Christ, and in the Bible, which witnessed to this revelation. Thus liberal Christianity, while refusing to deny values in this religion, found it necessary to place Jesus among the great rabbis and the Book among the documents of human inspiration. The sense of the *eph hapax*, the once-and-for-allness of the revelation, was obscured in the interest of eliding the Christian claim, making it less abrupt.

The critical tradition was not the only factor. In the latter half of the nineteenth century philosophical ideas of progress were happily conjoined with biological and scientific ideas of the evolution of nature and man. In such a sequence, Christianity was placed high on the escalator, as an outgrowth of an obsolete past but only as a stage toward a greater future. Because the intellectual assumptions of Christianity were challenged as they had not been since Greco-Roman times, sincere people who desired to keep the values of Christianity tended to downgrade the importance and uniqueness of the Person who was the bearer of the divine Word and the heart of revelation.

It would be inaccurate to say merely that the pendulum swung toward the end of the first quarter of the twentieth century. What happened was not so simple as that. It was not merely that men tired of pushing the idea of continuity so far that they became bored with it and invented new ideas in order to sell new books and gain new professorial prestige. Not at all. The shift came about on an utterly different basis. In the first place, the liberal idea bore within it the seeds of its own decay. The portrayal of Christianity that it fostered did not seem to be consistent with the *basic* claims the faith made in its own decisive revelation. Liberties were taken with those claims which could not permanently endure unless adherents of the faith should permit a transformation that would deny the past. Someone has said that you are free to draw a giraffe any way you wish, but that unless you draw it with a long neck and long legs, it will not be recognizable as a giraffe to anyone else. So in a sense you are not free: you are bound to draw it as it is.

So with the Christian faith. The short-necked, short-legged, spotless version of theology was an excellent example of adaptation to the low foliage of nineteenth-century naturalism. But it was not permanently recognizable as a witness to God's revelation in Jesus Christ. Therefore, from within, there was a sense of dissatisfaction.

External factors also had their place. First among these was the shattering of much of the nineteenth century's hopes through the events culminating in World War I. Although the previous century was never so shallow, overoptimistic, or blind in its faith in progress as later caricatures have made it out to be, even moderate views of progress were jolted by the catastrophe of 1914–1918. Placing Christianity on a continuum with the natural process made it impotent when the natural process itself offered little future and little hope. So, as a realistic reaction based on the empirics of the second decade of the century,

Christian theologians and laymen alike found it necessary to revise their hopes and to extricate the faith from the propriety of opinion in which it had come to be comfortable in the preceding years.

Although the change did not come about simply with the swinging of the pendulum, we might observe that once the pendulum picture is introduced we see that a swing did come and did swing too far. The instinctive reaction was to remove the entire liberal understanding, to deny all phases of the continuum, to stress the *un*naturalness of Christianity. In such a setting, the term "paradox" came into vogue to describe the content of the dialectical method in theology. Most of the men who played a role in the theological about-face found the term congenial and reintroduced it: Barth, Brunner, Gogarten, Thurneysen, and others among the Continental schools.

Now an entirely different feature was introduced. Some went so far as to elevate a dictum associated with Tertullian to an absolute theological principle (out of context): "I believe, because it is absurd; . . . it is certain, because it is impossible." Now the tendency was to deny points of contact between the divine and the human, the supernatural and the natural order, the infinite in its condescension in the finite. The absurd, the unnatural, the hiddenness of God (described as the Wholly Other) came to be stressed. As time passed, most of the thunderers against liberalism mellowed, learning again how much of its presupposition had validity and how much it had formed the thunderers themselves. So the idea of paradoxicality as being constitutive of theological method and content was also modified, and it is only this modified sense that shall be implied here.

"Paradox" has a distinctive Christian lineage. It is certainly a part of Paul's insistence in his first letter to the Corinthians that God, when he chooses to reveal himself, does not do so in the majesty associated with his glory. Instead, he comes in foolishness that is wiser than men; in the humble, the ignoble, even the "things that are not" to put to shame the things that are. This paradox rendered the Christian faith a stumbling block to the Jews, who had looked for the revelation on other terms, and a scandal to the Greeks, who would not see the possibility of the finite order's being interrupted by the infinite. Jesus, too, had often used the language of paradox: the greatest in the Kingdom must become like the child; he who would gain his life must lose it; only the grain of wheat that dies, lives; most of all, " He who believes in me, believes not in me but in him who sent me " (John 12:44).

In Christian history we confront this impropriety in Tertullian; in Nicolaus Cusanus' " learned ignorance " and in his idea of the coincidence of opposites. The Protestant Reformers worked with it with some consistency; Luther liked to stress the fact that we learn how things are going in the heavenly majesty only when we see the revelation in a gurgling, diapered baby or a dying man. God is hidden in his revelation *sub contraria specie*. The faith is expressed in apparently contradictory assertions. We are used to this approach again in the writings of Blaise Pascal (d.1662), who based it on the doctrine of man's Fall. This Fall limited man both rationally and morally; for God to contact him, there must be something contradictory in the manner of revelation. Contradictoriness becomes the key to human nature.

Recent theology has turned more to Sören Kierkegaard than to anyone else for elaborating the paradox. On the surface of things Kierkegaard seems to stand in the tradition of Tertullian, at least the Tertullian of caricature. On the surface he seems to say that Christian revelation goes contrary to reason and logic, that it violates normal human categories of discourse. Yet Kierkegaard means something other than this:

> It is the duty of the human understanding to understand that there are things which it cannot understand, and what those things are. Human understanding has vulgarly occupied itself with nothing but understanding, but if it would only take the trouble to understand itself at the same time, it would simply have to posit the paradox. The paradox is not a concession but

a category, an ontological definition which expresses the relation between an existing cognitive spirit and eternal truth.[6]

Of this kind of talk Kierkegaard student Martin Heinecken
has written:

> It is really quite amazing why anyone should seriously object to
> the admission of such a possibility and should condemn it as a
> cult of irrationalism. . . . All that is meant is that a man should
> admit he is confronted with something the intellect cannot
> handle, and how else could he be persuaded more convincingly
> than by means of the absolute paradox?[7]

So it was not Kierkegaard's intention to place paradox under
the idea of irrationality but to assign to it a category. The decisions of faith were not made contrary to reason but were
made in "the passions." This is reminiscent of Pascal's "The
heart has its reasons which reason knows nothing of."

In the twentieth century these ideas were picked up by Emil
Brunner, who with Pascal placed paradox under the terms of
man's self-contradiction because of the Fall; man is the creature
who is both aware of his contradiction and yet at the same
time denies it. Similarly, it was seen to be part of the nature of
revelation by Karl Barth:

> We can only speak of the glory of God in creation as we bring
> out the complete hiddenness of God for our eyes in nature; of
> the image of God in man only as we give warning once for all
> that the man we know is fallen; of sin, only with the reminder
> that we should not know sin, were it not forgiven of us; of the
> justification of the ungodly, only as we recall that it is the un-
> godly who is declared just.[8]

Few contemporary theologians or preachers have wholly es-
caped the influence of ideas like these, whether or not they have
arrived at them for similar reasons but independently of Barth
and his colleagues. Often those who protest most loudly that
they are independent of the influence are most obviously
formed theologically in relation to it. There is no doubt but

that future histories of the theology of our time will have to deal to a large extent with the reintroduction of the category of paradox.

However, it is not our interest here to write a tract in defense of the dialectical theology (which we have no desire to do) or to elaborate it (which we are incapable of doing). Instead, in a book on mass media, it is worth-while for tactical reasons to stage a strategic retreat. Instead of seeing how far the category of paradox can be pushed, let us see how necessary it appears even for a minimal statement of the "foolishness of God," which is the scandal of Christian particularity.

Here we see that the more extreme theologians have done the term and perhaps the faith a disservice by making it seem as if Christianity is a cult of irrationality. On this point I agree with W. Norman Pittenger: it is hard enough to be a Christian; there is no point in making it more difficult than it need be. There is nothing gained in denying points of continuity, in refusing to build bridges or to see parallels between Christianity and its background or culture. Thus, Christianity is sometimes unnecessarily dismissed when it is claimed that paradox means "contrary to reason." For our minimal restorative task, we can begin with the dictionary.

"Paradox" is there (*Webster's New International Dictionary*) defined as that which is contrary not to reason but to opinion. "A tenet or proposition contrary to received opinion; also, an assertion or sentiment seemingly contradictory, or opposed to common sense, but that yet may be true in fact." *Doxa* means not "reason" but "opinion"; its root is *dokein*, "to suppose" or "imagine." It is on this ground that Paul Tillich has done the faith a service in his own apologetic work. Seeking to correlate theology with philosophy and other disciplines, he is offended by those who would overoffend in the cult of irrationality.

Theological dialectics, says Tillich, does not violate the principle of logical rationality. Paul's *paradoxa* (referred to above) are not illogical. He is giving understandable and logical expression to the infinite tensions of Christian existence. Nor (and here Tillich argues with Emil Brunner explicity) does John intend something illogical when he speaks of the Word's becoming flesh. All these words are attempts to express the conviction that God's action transcends human expectations and preparations. It transcends but does not violate reason.

> The term " paradox " should be defined carefully, and paradoxical language should be used with discrimination. Paradoxical means " against the opinion," namely, the opinion of finite reason. . . . There is, in the last analysis, only *one* genuine paradox in the Christian message — the appearance of that which conquers existence under the conditions of existence. Incarnation, redemption, justification, etc., are implied in this paradoxical event. . . . Paradox has its logical place.[9]

In the second volume of the *Systematic Theology*, Tillich relates the paradox to "Existence and the Christ"; there he contradistinguishes it from the reflective-rational, the absurd, and the nonsensical.

> That is paradoxical which contradicts the *doxa*, the opinion which is based on the whole or ordinary human experience, including the empirical and the rational. The Christian paradox contradicts the opinion derived from man's existential predicament and all expectations imaginable on the basis of this predicament. The " offense " given by the paradoxical character of the Christian message is not against the laws of understandable speech but *against man's ordinary interpretation of his predicament* with respect to himself, his world, and the ultimate underlying both of them. . . . The paradox is a new reality and not a logical riddle.[10] [Emphasis mine.]

For Tillich, then, " historically and systematically, everything else in Christianity is a corroboration of the simple assertion that Jesus is the Christ."

In other contexts I should be as interested in enlarging on Tillich's minimum, his analogy from the single paradox, as I am here in resting content with it. For the moment, in a discussion of mass media of communication, I too want to wear the apologist's mantle, to " go about as far as one can go."

What seems to be consistent in both absurd and minimal discussions of the Christian paradox is this: the revelation of God in Jesus Christ goes against "man's ordinary interpretation of his predicament." Mass media, by their very nature, must normally propagate normal, ordinary, and proper interpretations of that predicament, whether on nonreligious or religious lines. There are varieties of theological constructs for approaching this turning point of my whole argument. For me the infinite/finite dialect is most meaningful: on the classic lines of the Lutheran Reformation there is interest in the concreteness of revelation. *Finitum capax infiniti:* the finite is capable of bearing the infinite in its condescension. The Roman Catholic in his theology of merit and grace ordinarily prefers the supernatural/natural poles. Just as good. Much of the more liberal Protestant theology prefers transcendent/immanent as congenial categories.

As a matter of fact, one who might be reluctant to use any of them still must deal with the ways in which the Christian revelation interrupts man's normal preparation and expectation. Thus Albert Outler:

> Ten years ago, as I can see by my lecture notes, I was still belaboring traditional phrases — rational and irrational, natural and supernatural, transcendent and immanent, finite and infinite — as metaphors about God and the world. Aided by Biblical theologians I have come to see that this split-level language does not ring true in terms of the Bible or Christian experience. I have come to believe that it is better to begin with the fact that God is *always* present and acting, whether " known " or not. Then one can speak of the two different ways that he is present: either in his mystery or his manifestation. God-Mysterious is utterly ineffable; God-Manifest is actually knowable, but only when, where, and as he chooses to reveal himself. We are aware of God-Mysterious — and this awareness is as primitive as our awareness of motion, causality, or self. We are also grasped by the presence of God-Manifest, and this supplies the data of religious knowledge. In neither case is God at our disposal.[11]

Whether in the cult of irrationality, or in the reduction of all paradox to one transcendence of opinion, or in the translation that Biblical theology effects, we are at the same point. Only in the ultimate liberal reduction (remember the picture of the giraffe) is Christianity capable of being "the proper opinion" for people who communicate through or respond to the media on nonreligious or religious terms. This fact has profound implications for the interpreting of the media and for their use by Christians for a nonselective readership or audience.

It is not a logical contradiction to say that mass media can serve to form the improper opinion that Christian revelation implies. Not at all. Here too, the idea we might say is paradoxical; that is, it goes beyond normal expectations. Perhaps this is what has generated so much hope and so many investments by those who in the name of Christianity would use the media for conversionist reasons rather than for nurture. It is always theoretically possible that a majority of the mass would find the scandal of Christian particularity acceptable, that it would still respond and purchase the product that goes with the offense.

As a point of interest, the mass media have been singularly successful in promoting the irrational as opposed to the paradoxical. The racial agitator in the American South has long known how easy it is to upset the delicate balances of reason carefully built up over the years by an evening's misuse of a rumor in a newspaper or over television. A Negro family may move into a new area of a Northern city, and nothing really or rationally happens to property. But mass communicators, by the way they report or propagate rumor, can in a matter of minutes stir up a mass of people to the kind of insecurity that makes possible the irrational: home values go down because someone of a different color occupies one.

Nor is it necessary to enlarge on the fact that just as the ideologist does, so the advertiser knows the effectiveness of the irrational in the mass media. The deception in so much advertising, the play upon anxieties and worries, the promise of earthly paradises on painless installment plans — most of these gambits are basically irrational in their appeal. Yet they are successful. And the demagogue who would control needs nothing so much as he does a mass audience to effect what he could not achieve in quiet dialogue with another person. Hitler's technique of " the big lie "; Senator McCarthy's approach, " the big insinuation "; Fidel Castro's method, the inexhaustible larynx used in harangue — these demonstrate all too well that one need not shy away from presenting the irrational over mass media or on the printed page with expectations of success.

But it is not the irrational that the Christian would present, and in the name of Christianity we must protest every ideological use of the media. We must protest all appeals of a commercial type that would sell Christianity by misusing the people it would convert. Nor is there room for the demagogic leading of people, making them what Eric Hoffer calls " True Believers " in the name of a faith that would relate persons to a Person. It is a quieter paradox that is to be offered — and its assumption, transcending both categories of reason and of unreason, has a unique place in the matter of mass response.

The Christian gospel has a universal intention: " God so loved *the world* . . . ; God was in Christ reconciling *the world* to himself " (John 3:16; II Cor. 5:19). Perhaps it may even have a universal outcome. But in the categories of humanness — substance and causality, time and space — here its promise and its demand interrupt " man's ordinary interpretations of his predicament " (Tillich). Reverend Father, that is too much! This book is written because of faith in the possibility that mass media can do something for the Christian faith. What can be communicated to one person can also be beamed to many — the important question is how to do it meaningfully, effectively, and in consistency with the Christian claim. Here I am arguing that to a large, nonselective audience, the Christian's best use of mass media is not a head-on, direct, frontal assault. In this context we can see some of the difficulties if we explore certain extensions of what Tillich has called the one paradox.

As an instance, begin with the idea of a mass-magazine article on the Christian witness to the living God of creation. The theologian or preacher or scientist who has the opportunity to present this as an option in a contribution to interfaith discussions has it easy. But it is scarcely conceivable that a magazine of mass circulation would commit itself permanently to the portrayal of the God of creation in religious terms. For it to do so would violate the propriety of opinion that advertisers seek to cultivate. The problem is doubly complicated by the fact that the mythical readership would include people who bring to the article both nonreligious and religious suppositions. The reader of the scientific journals or, for that matter, anyone shaped subtly by the scientific world view would have difficulty in clothing himself with the " myth " that makes a Christian assertion possible. If he is to find God via creation, a frontal proclamation of this fact is meaningless.

Not so with the religious person. He (if he is an average American) believes in God. Either he has proved this belief to himself or he intuits it. But the God at which he has arrived is undoubtedly different from the God of the Christian faith. There is no question but that he should be confronted with Christian particularity; but the magazine publisher is not going to permit extended and isolated discussions of the Christian view because of the hazard to his readership. For the doctrine of Creation is offensive too.

Witness to the God of creation runs counter to human expectation. We would expect to find God with some confidence and clarity in his created order. We are disappointed to find that Christianity does not provide that kind of knowledge on those terms. What kind of God is it, that he can so successfully cover up his traces, that knowledge of him gained from his works is almost meaningless? So we naturally turn to the more comfortable gods that we can find.

The moment we entertain the idea of Christian witness against such gods, we run into a host of practical problems. Who is the Christian who is speaking? Is he a naturalist or a

supernaturalist, a Roman Catholic, a Protestant, a fundamentalist? For whichever he is, he will tend to cancel other options.
The Roman Catholic will tell the reader to find the God of
creation authoritatively revealed in the church. But already the
sense of the article has shifted. The fundamentalist will shout
for the authority of the Book. But how to be drawn to its power
is already so great a mystery for the nonreligious or the usual
religious reader that the article will lose him at that point.

Proofs for the existence of God are of little help except to
clear away debris. The more intelligent reader knows that these
proofs are so suspect within the church that he scarcely need
entertain them from the outside. He may have concluded that
God *is,* but he is nowhere near the knowledge of *who* God is.
And when he is told, head on, that the God of creation who
upholds all things (and he knows a good deal about "all
things" and their scope) chooses to be known definitively in
the man Christ Jesus, he cancels out. The Christian tends to
"back up" into his view of creation through Jesus Christ. This
is not a very meaningful way of approaching the idea of creation to people for whom Christianity is not yet an option.

A second example: the temptation for Christianity to degenerate into religiousness when it uses mass media to communicate is clear from the tendency to moralize the situation of
man at such times. There is no need at this late date for us to
suggest that Christianity has a monopoly in describing the
grandeur and misery of man. But it does have a difference in
the context in which it places these dimensions of man's nature,
and that makes all the difference. The reader of a newspaper
scarcely needs to be told that man can be charitable: the modern metropolitan press has often shown an almost sentimental
tendency to thaw the hardheartedness and coldness of modern
people into acts of charity. He does not need to be told that
man is capable of being hateful and degrading; this, too, is clear
from the daily record of the headlines. So when the Christian
comes along and says, in the religio-moralistic terms of the
motto, "There is so much good in the worst of us, and so much

bad in the best of us, that it hardly becomes any of us to talk
about the rest of us," the notion is capable of being absorbed
among the proper opinions of the day.

Something else comes into play, however, the moment the
Christian paradox is introduced. Now, the definition of the
grandeur of man is established, but not in the light of original
perfection; instead, " man is the creature made visible in the
mirror of Jesus Christ," a particular Man. Here the offense begins to come into play. Why Jesus? Why not Mohammed or
Maimonides or Gandhi? Even more, it offends the commonly
held view of the accidental or environmental character of the
human predicament to be told that something about man is
now substantially different. One may read a newspaper account
in which a sermon is reported on in the most open terms. Such
a sermon could have spoken of the corruptness of man. It could
be dismissed as interesting but idiosyncratic.

It would be unthinkable, however, for a metropolitan newspaper to make a standard policy of analyzing the situation of
man in the light of God's event in Jesus Christ. A newspaper
that originates within the Christian community and is directed
toward it may regularly introduce this dimension. But in the
secular press such an assumption would be meaningless.

So the nonreligious world goes about its business analyzing
man with great profundity. *Death of a Salesman* or a Pulitzer
Prize reporting of a national scandal may be more on target
than many shallow and thoughtless Christian sermons. It may
dangle some sort of paradise before men. The promise of suburbia and the new automobile parked in front of a club are
actually more vivid than many a portrayal of the Christian
promise in terms of a meaningless stretch of boring Sunday-
afternoon kind of everlastingness and harp-playing apathy. But
both the analysis and the promise must occur within a circumscribed context that the Christian seeks to interrupt. And he is
tempted to do this in moralistic terms: let us all do our best.
This is a comforting teaching, a marketable view of man's
creaturehood, his self-contradiction, his redemption. It offends

no one. But it has nothing to do with Christianity's unpopular opinion about man's nature and destiny. The newspaper provides a poor outlet for that opinion on a massive scale.

God and man meet in history, and history is the stuff also of good fiction. This is the plane where things matter. The form of the best-selling novel should be an excellent vehicle to propagate the Christian faith. But if the faith is presented in its authentic form — as that which violates man's preconceptions of his predicament and its solution — it is not intelligible as a mass option, particularly if the presentation is made explicitly and frontally.

Actually, the novel commends itself better than most other forms of mass communication for this purpose. It is a more selective medium; it involves pacing and longer commitment to its destiny. Christians have learned to present the faith in history in this form. Today one thinks of such men as Graham Greene, Joyce Cary, Evelyn Waugh, and Alan Paton. But their method is intuitive and almost insinuating; their view of history is complex and their path to Christian destiny circuitous. The impotence of the " Christian " novel couched in explicit terms is clear from the artistic and emotional deadness of the religious novels produced for denominational consumption. We would be hard put to remember the name or the plot of any one of the many that have crossed our desk in the last decade.

What is wrong with most such portrayals of a Christian view of history is this: there is a too-cozy identification with providence. " God " brings boys and girls together, and we have romance. " God " sends men out to adventure and saves them in shipwreck. Since our times are in " God's " hands, all comes out well in the end, after the appropriate span of melodrama and tears. And the reader knows: this is not how things work.

The nonreligious reader dismisses it all as a masquerade, an attempt to present a meaningless *mythos*. Obviously, God does not interrupt this order, with its shell fire and malignant cells and accidents of meeting and parting. The religious reader expects more than can be delivered: he wants the good fortune of moral man to be applied to him, no questions asked. He knows that God is not only relatively *absconditus* as the "someone in the great somewhere" but also *revelatus* as the "Man upstairs" who is at his beck and call. The Christian view of history goes too far for a person of secular orientation and falls short of religious expectation.

For the Christian believes, indeed, that God does have to do with history. He believes that the God of creation does not abandon his creature. But this God does not give satisfying religious explanations of the problem of evil in history or of the promise of good beyond it. Instead, he participates in history; he bridges the gap in the incarnation. The nonreligious person asks why history is made meaningful at all in this particular event and not in some other. Why should the revelation be made among the Jews in 4 B.C. and not among the Maoris or Manhattanites of later date? The religious person asks why history is made meaningful only in this particular scandal and not in a generalized way among good men. The Christian says, not "onward and upward," but, "I live by the faith of the Son of God." That God reveals himself to men in wrath and condescends in a Person — that is too much. Later we shall see some of the ways this can be told in the mass media; now we are only suggesting the limits of explicit revelation in this form.

If we wish to see in sharpest contrast the difference between what Christianity asks and offers and what mass media imply, we can juxtapose the central Christian teaching, relating to the death and resurrection of Jesus Christ, to the most inclusive medium, television. Now all appears in bold outlines. Television's audience is much less selective than is the readership of the printed page; it is difficult to scan. So producers of television, because of the need for efficiency in an expensive medium, ask for inclusive subjects to be presented in an inoffensive manner. The familiar instance here is that of the commercial sponsor who shuns controversial material.

It is possible to domesticate the atonement, to present it in cozy and comfortable terms. It can be reduced to formulas

("Jesus saves"; "Are you saved?") that are blunt and explicit but scarcely demand levels of intensity and awareness. The figure of Jesus can be prettified so that his suffering appears in the familiar Monophysite cast. In these senses, there is room on the inclusive kinetic medium for portrayal of the events symbolized in the term "atonement."

Most explicit reference to the central Christian mystery occurs in one of three ways. First, it may be a private proclamation to a private segment of the audience. Much of the preaching that is safely tucked away on a Sunday morning falls into this category. It is almost inconceivable that anyone from "the mass" will be touched by this. Second, there is the somewhat larger opportunity presented because stations must offer time as a public service. Here national organizations sometimes have opportunity to state their case responsibly. The third familiar pattern occurs on holidays when, in pageant, service, or song, the Christian event is pondered, sometimes by substantial audiences. It can happen.

Several factors militate against the frequency or effectiveness of its happenings. One of these is understandable: a large part of the control of television is in New York, a power center impressively dominated and staffed by people of nonreligious or of Jewish orientation. There is no point in regretting this situation: it is just how things are, and one expects assertions of Christian particularity from such an elite no more than one would expect Christians to go out of their way to propound Jewish dogma or secular creeds. The situation is further complicated by the varieties of Christian witness to the event: will Roman Catholic piety in its concentration on the sufferings of Christ satisfy Protestants, some of whom stress the triumph of the resurrection and some of whom make of the atonement largely an event of moral influence?

If we strip the atonement of the formulas that popular evangelism uses as slogans and really reflect on its meaning, it runs counter to propriety. Unless presented with the whole Christian construct, it may well fall under the classic condemnation:

it may undercut morality. " I like to commit sins. God likes to forgive them. Really, the world is admirably arranged." The person of secular orientation dismisses the central Christian teaching as meaningless in its formulas. The religious person is offended by the way it counters normal human aspirations. The moralist is concerned lest cheap grace subvert society.

As we think about it, none of us *naturally* is at home with the idea of God's initiative. None of us is sure we understand what it means that in Christ he accepts the unacceptable. None of us can domesticate the paradox, to return to Tillich's terms — " the appearance of that which conquers existence under the conditions of existence." As Luther has said, the teaching about the forgiveness of sins is potentially comforting — but it is also mighty dangerous. The more reflective children of the world often see that more readily than do the contented and settled Christians. For the declaration of grace as a result of the atonement is a last resort; it occurs after man's moral quest is exhausted. It is a costly grace. And thirty minutes of prime-time television seldom provide the context in which this can be presented in a manner beyond the conventional and formulistic.

Perhaps in this survey of conflicts the impression has been given that the secular order is itself to blame for all the ills that plague Christian communication through mass media. Not at all. With a slight shift in emphasis it is possible to see how an intra-Christian situation serves to complicate the presentation of the faith. The illustration that immediately comes to mind is the approach to the doctrine of the church presented over radio.

None of the media has been seized upon so eagerly for mass portrayal of Christianity as has radio. But in no other instance is the welter of competing claims within Christianity made so deadeningly clear as it is in radio. Not only do countless small voices find it possible to broadcast sectarian and divisive words, but even on the highest levels of unity, the variety that radio provides shows particularity to have gone askew.

This is the dilemma of the radiobroadcaster: he presents

Christ as the hope of the world and the church as his body. Somehow this fellowship of finite and sinful mortals is part of God's condescension. Yet the listener, if he is aware, knows that this body is not one but apparently many. It presents itself to him as a confusion of competitive, self-seeking members — also on the radio. The proper opinion for the respectable person would be that such a shortsighted organism or institution should be avoided. The popular idea of religion permits communion on the golf course and allows morality to be determined in solitariness.

The Christian faith does not leave man alone at this point. Although not all Christians will go so far as to assert that outside the church there is no salvation, they all speak of the essentiality of the church to the fullness of faith. It is offensive indeed to point to such a divided, imperfect, publicly failing fellowship and to say: In spite of what you see, here too God acts mightily. Radiobroadcasting in the hands of religious agencies has the further difficulty that it enters so many living rooms and autos it creates the impression that salvation is an individual affair and an autonomous decision. The Christian faith is classically expressed as a corporate and attracting agent. In the interest of building up community, its many voices tend to pull it down.

When motion-picture producers decide to be fair to religion, they find it necessary to compete for the attention of people in this most democratic art. They have created numbers of utopias and now, in justice, they want to present the religious hope. Yet the mythology of the afterlife in motion pictures has been notoriously removed from the Christian hope; any attempt to describe *seriously* (i.e., above the level of folklore, as in *Green Pastures* and its imitators) the nature of God's salvation and the kind of exclusivism associated with Christianity's uniqueness brings about a loss of mass understanding.

The proper opinion says that in some vague future I shall receive some vague reward. The Christian's improper view is that, despite what I have been, my life is hid with Christ in

God. And God is faithful, holding promise for the life that is and that is to come. The film producer who would make standard fare of the serious Christian claim will soon have an enthusiastic following in the churches but he will have a private, directed medium and not one that can be related to the mass.

These are all variations on a single theme: nonreligious and religious audiences, readers, or markets have carefully succeeded in insulating themselves against the Christian paradox and its analogies. This insulation must somehow be torn away or worn away if the Christian message is to have effect. Mass media can be an instrument in this task. But at every decisive point a frontal, explicit presentation is frustrated by the nature of the medium it is using. Formal and open exposure is successful when directed to the already convinced. Other ways must be found for presenting and interpreting Christianity effectively there where ideas are marketed.

Chapter IV

The Forms of Christian Presentation

Until now we have left an impression that communication of the Christian faith through mass media is virtually impossible. The impression is not entirely accurate. Although difficult, such communication is not beyond the range of the possible. The critique that preceded was itself deficient in that it was partial. It concerned itself almost entirely with what we called formal, frontal, head-on, explicit, and direct confrontation of an audience or a readership. Such has been the usual approach, and it accounts for much of the failure. But this is not the only approach. Mass communication ought to offer to the Christian community the richness of opportunity and the variety of textures that the Christian message has always found open to it in every age — and more!

For the task that is ahead, "communication" is a rather inadequate term. Although it appears from time to time because of its place in normal discourse, it represents here a " cheating " word. It dangles before the reader a possibility that does not exist. For communication is a two-way street, whether in living room or correspondence. And the mass media do not really provide for dialogue except in the indirect sense of reader response ("Letters to the Editor ") or the subtler, silent affirmations or negations that pollsters can count. The quest for a better word need go no farther than the New Testament. Call it, fairly, the presentation of the faith. The Greek root is *paristanein* (*par-*

istanai). (In several instances the Revised Standard Version translates words of other roots as " present "; in each case they are apropos and further substantiate the case for the English term even where they have complex Greek origins. Thus, Acts 17:19 refers to *teaching:* " May we know what this new teaching is which you present? " [*hypo sou laloumenē*]. A glorious instance parallel to Rom. 12:1, " Present your bodies as a living sacrifice," is in Jude 24, "Now to him who is able to keep you from falling and to *present* you without blemish before the presence of his glory with rejoicing" [*stēsai*].) Instantly the manifoldness of the faith finds expression, each aspect of it applicable to the mass media. In the New Testament it includes the presentation of Christ, his teaching, his people.

In several instances *paristanein* refers to Christ, whether as infant, presented in the Temple at the time of the purification (Luke 2:22), or as glorified, presented by himself alive after his Passion by many proofs (Acts 1:3). More often it applies to the presentation of the Christian self or the church as the people of God. The classic instance is the injunction to present one's self as a living sacrifice to God; a parallel is II Cor. 11:2 where the church is compared to the betrothed who is being presented as a pure bride to her husband. Similarly, in Eph. 5:27 the church is presented in splendor. Paul, writing to the Colossians (ch. 1:29), speaks of the energy that goes into " presenting every man mature in Christ." The stress in II Tim. 2:15 is again on the presentation of the Christian self to God. At the same time, the word refers to the presentation of the fruits of Christian work to the eyes of men, as in Acts 9:41, where Peter raises Dorcas and makes the act public by " presenting her alive " to the saints and widows.

The virtue of the word in this usage is its double application to Christ and to his people and the fact that in each instance it involves some sort of offering in suffering or in glory, that the public activity of God may be made known. There is always a certain self-conscious activity involved, some sense of the divesting of mystery through ritual or publicity. The person wears a variety of masks, however authentic they may be, and each reveals (as it conceals) personhood.

Erving Goffman has given the word a full-ranged modern usage in a dissertation, *The Presentation of Self in Everyday Life*.[12]

Here is a one-way act that sets the terms for later communication. Although it originates with the person behind the mask, it inspires or initiates human interaction along lines of certain prescriptions. Goffman cites Santayana on masks as " arrested expressions and admirable echoes of feeling, at once faithful, discreet, and superlative." He speaks with favor of these masks; they are like the cuticle that living things in contact with the air must acquire; one must not be angry with images for not being things. " Words and images are like shells, no less integral parts of nature than are the substances they cover, but *better addressed to the eye and more open to observation*." Thus substance and appearance, face and mask, passion and poetry, are equally involved in the round of existence.

The implications of this fact for mass media will become clear as we discern the necessities of self-conscious presentation in masks, appearances, and poetry. Goffman sees human activity as a theatrical performance, somewhat stylized and image-centered. The communication known as presentation has a promissory character; it tends to tantalize and to offer more than it can deliver, but what it offers can be honest. Ordinarily the presentation is an initial definition (page 12) of the situation projected by an individual to provide a plan for the cooperative activity that follows. There is immense value in this promissory and preliminary activity. Thus Robert Park:

> It is probably no mere historical accident that the word " person," in its first meaning, is a mask. It is rather a recognition of the fact that everyone is always and everywhere, more or less consciously, playing a role. . . . It is in these roles that we know each other; it is in these roles that we know ourselves.

In a sense, and in so far as this mask represents the conception we have formed of ourselves — the role we are striving to live up to — this mask is our truer self, the self we would like to be. In the end, our conception of our role becomes second nature and an integral part of our personality. We come into the world as individuals, achieve character, and become persons.[13]

We are leading up to this: the presentation of the faith through the mask of the media, although immensely difficult, may hold out entirely new possibilities for Christianity, yet possibilities consistent with classic activity. But it will look different; there will be less room for the unmasked, head-on confrontation at the distance and with the remoteness the media must imply.

Goffman is certainly not unaware of the dangers of misrepresentation and contrivance. But he alerts us to a moral side of this image-projection, the necessity of having to live up to what the promissory and the preliminary presentation suggested. In their roles as performers, individuals will be concerned with maintaining the impression that they live up to the standards by which they and their products are judged. "Because these standards are so numerous and so pervasive, the individuals who are performers dwell more than we might think in a moral world."

To use a different imagery, the very obligation and profitability of appearing always in a steady moral light, of being a socialized character, forces one to be the sort of person who is practiced in the ways of the stage.

The mask is not the only form for initiating communication; "scaffolds, after all, are to build other things with, and should be so erected with an eye to taking them down" (page 254). So in our quest for a new charter in presenting the faith through new media we shall be conscious of the need to point to the promissory and preliminary character of the presentation. But this preparation for the gospel is itself a worthy work in the Christian vocational community and in this light can offer opportunities that men and women now involved in projecting it frontally seldom dream of.

We can carry this quest a step farther and see ways in which the faster-paced, less-enduring, less-selective, and more kinetic media, which until now have seemed to fall under more consistent criticism, have special assets for this work. Whoever has lived with motion pictures or television knows the popular appeal they hold. Although intellectuals may almost automatically defend an original book as being superior to a derivative motion picture, they sense the ways the burden of proof has shifted in their direction. They seem to be under some sort of compulsion to justify their preference for the more static and reflective media. They may be haunted by their minority status, by a foreboding that they are living in an era that may make their preferences obsolete. The Jesuit scholar Walter Ong has presented this most chillingly: "In the age of television, voice is in some ways regaining a prestige over sight. . . . We are at the end of the Gutenberg era."

Father Ong, as the prophet of Gutenberg's demise, opened new doors to this possibility in a little-publicized essay in *Thought* called "Voice as Summons for Belief."[14] Here the text is from Ambrose: "Everything that we believe, we believe either through sight or through hearing. Sight is often deceived, hearing serves as guaranty." (*Commentary on St. Luke*, Book IV, chap. v.) This defense of the speaking presentation also has New Testament warrant: if those who believe without seeing are blessed, even more, "faith cometh by hearing." If belief is to be engendered, voice is an excellent instrument but it is masked. Ong argues: Why is the invitation more insistent when the speaker wears a mask? Because human persons are of themselves distant from one another in that they cannot enter entirely into one another's consciousness. The other person is always partly unfathomable to me. But voice "is the least exterior of sensible phenomena because it emanates not only from the physical but also from the divided psychological interior of man and penetrates to another physical and psychological interior where, as we have seen, it must be re-created in the imagination in order to live." But even a voice is an exterior something. Here is where the mask appears in dramatic performance and through analogy, in literature. It stands for all that in the person-to-person situation which is nonvocal, noncommunicative, nonpersonal, remote, alienated.

Ong discusses some of the dramatic break-throughs, particularly the one that is heightened in Christian history, where God concerns himself with human history and appears in personal fashion (though he is known through a mask of faith, as " through a glass darkly "). Most of all he appears in the second Person of the Trinity who is not only Word but also Son. All God's works now come through masks, including the water, the bread and the wine of the Sacrament, and the activity of the Christian community. The Word is connected with these; and voice remains, through the mask, a summons for belief. It is this summons that is longed for in an age of insecurity and rootlessness; and, if Ong is correct, our age has in many ways compensated for the depersonalizing that goes on:

> There is no doubt in our age, which has evolved, among other things, a mass culture and mass media of communication, intimacy is also in many ways better served than it has ever been before. Certainly the human race is more conscious of itself as a whole and has developed its dialogue about intimacy and communication more than at earlier periods in human history. ... The philosophy known as personalism is a twentieth-century creation, just as thoroughly a product of our age as technology or television commercials. In this climate belief *in* becomes very meaningful. (Page 61.)

If we accept this view of voice as summons for belief and for the presentation of the self to a mass through a mask, we begin to realize many of the bases for change in our life. I shall use two illustrations.

First is the example of the recovery of private confession. Most of Protestant Christianity tended to minimize the value

of the act and because of its association with the merit system
of Roman Catholicism, had tended to reject or neglect it. Magazine articles recently have devoted themselves to the recovery
of such confession. Many have seen it to have not only "sacramental" value but also in a more normally medical sense a
therapeutic value; it satisfies many longings in our day. Is not
part of the effectiveness of private confession inherent in the
fact that in it I am confronted by a representative person who
presents himself as one who accepts through the mask of ministry or priesthood? The activity of a forgiving God becomes
meaningful when the voice of another is addressed to me.

> Assurance that the confession is being made to a person wise
> and experienced in life can be of great importance in some
> cases. Naturally, one confesses to a person of understanding
> who will listen in the right manner; but an individual who has
> failed often wants to feel that he is confessing to "a real human
> being" in order to be sure, when the "arms of humanity are
> opened to him" again, that the sense of forgiveness he feels is
> real beyond question because the person through whom it has
> been mediated has the breadth of knowledge and depth of ex-
> perience needed to apprehend the full significance of all that
> has been disclosed. . . .
> He will feel his need of someone who is at once a real human
> being and a Christian; a true representative of the spiritual
> fellowship against which he has sinned.[15]

This self-evident psychological phenomenon is itself a reaffir-
mation of a classic Christian insight into sin and forgiveness.

The second illustration is more directly related to the problem of mass communication and has to do with the nature of
the Word, which is the summons for belief. On two levels, extension of the Word into human life through the Book has
become more difficult. On one, the popular level, there is the
familiar complaint that although Bible distribution is at an all-
time high level — near saturation in the "Christian" world —
Biblical illiteracy is alarming. All of us have heard hoary sermons in which the preacher tells of dust-covered Bibles that

serve only as keepsakes. The purchase of Bibles seems to be motivated by good intentions and is viewed as an act of piety, but the gap between purchase and eager readership is wide. Often there is perfunctory fulfillment of the promise of the Book through laborious carrying out of " Bible-reading plans."

That this situation is far removed from the years when first the printing press made possible extensive distribution of Bibles is obvious. It is difficult today to recapture the spirit of newness that was created by this publication; the ferments and revolutions that it generated are virtually unthinkable today. Today the Book as object may have sacramental or fetishistic value but its newness (not novelty, but the inherent dynamism and creative power of the Word) is less dramatic.

On the second level, Biblical scholarship has shown mistrust of the power of the Book. This may look to the outsider as if the scholarly community is, as they say, cutting off its nose to spite its own face. Who should be more interested in the persuasive power of the page than the intellectual or theological community? Yet one of the consistent efforts of modern theological pursuit has been the insistence on separating Word of God from printed page. The Word of God is seen again as the activity of Him who " lays bare his holy arm." It is seen in the utterances of the prophets, the mighty acts of the kings; in the words and works of apostles and evangelists, and most of all in the man of God's own choosing through whom he speaks in the latter days. The Bible is seen as the witness to this activity, as the living document that safeguards the intactness of the message. But the apparent downgrading of the power of the page is disturbing. In the desire to show that " Word of God " is not exhausted when we have said " Bible," there is the danger that we shall fail to see that God has also chosen this instrument for his voice.

But if we ask why there is an effort at recovering the vocal dynamism of the Word that produces faith at the expense of the revered but unread page, we touch on some profound chords of our industrial age. When we agree with Luther that

the church is not a "book house" but a "mouth house" and
that the Word is not so much *geschrieben* (written) but *ge-schrieen* (shouted), we are saying much about ourselves. Frequently I have heard this emphasis described as a romantic
aversion to the Book. It is true that the Romantic period,
heightened by the nineteenth-century reaction to an industrial
society, reacted against the deadening effect of print. The
poets who depended upon the printed page lived with the
illusion that they could deny this.

We have, however, now passed from the Romantic period
to another stage of civilization and, though the afterglow may
be here, we are now part of a disillusioned and often cynical
twentieth century. Why, then, the downgrading of the Book?
Here the clue given us before may be availing: we may be
entering the end of the age of Gutenberg and the time of the
more kinetic and dynamic media. This does not mean that the
end of the production of printed pages is near or to us even
yet conceivable (though many prophets of the electronic era
have offered this forecast), but the relative power of the page
directed to the millions is limited in the years when world-wide
instantaneous audio-visual projection through television is a
near-possibility. Study of the Book may be intense, but it is in
many ways the pursuit of a specialized community. The many
attempts to render the Bible accessible to "the Common
Reader" suggest the way the burden of proof has shifted, for
the *koinē* language of the New Testament and the reconciling
power of God that breaks through the pages have always meant
that the Bible was *only* for the common reader.

This subject holds tantalizing possibilities and perplexing
problems for us. I do not despair over the future of the Book,
and I believe that certain theological and psychological assumptions provide new possibilities, which those of us who love
it could pursue. This subject would lead us astray from the
current development of argument, however. For now it remains
only a part of the cultural setting in which Biblical scholars
themselves stress less the printed page. They stress more the

acts of God, the Word of God in Christ, the word of the Christian community, the living witness today. In a depersonalizing and dehumanizing age we long for intimacy with the other while preserving our own integrity from annihilation. We pursue this longing by listening to another voice, which makes it possible to participate in or to see an exchange with the interior life of the other one. The voice is mediated through the mask which, back to Goffman's term, involves the presentation of the self. This self-presentation is what gives preaching part of the psychological power it retains in a day notable for the lack of theological content in so many sermons. This is what gives personal counseling and personal confession its place in the remembered rubrics of the church's life. This is what makes the media that project not only words but voices and faces so powerful today. This is what forces upon the community of those who care the necessity for countering the proper opinions (belief *that*) with Christianity's improper opinion (belief *in*).

This view of revelation through the mask (classically expressed as the concept of the *larvae Dei*) illumines the problem of the previous chapter: the relative impotence of frontal, head-on announcement of Christian particularity to a mass audience. In its frontality it is somehow unmediated through the masks of credibility. Goffman in his study does not go far enough in pursuit of the question of credibility. What happens when the mask is unrecognizable even if authentic? The madman in Nietzsche's *Joyful Wisdom* senses this failure about his own prophecies. He runs out on a bright morning with a lighted lantern, and in the market place shouts: " I seek God! "

As there were many people standing about who did not believe in God, he caused a great deal of amusement. Why! Is he lost? said one. Has he strayed away like a child? said another. Or does he keep himself hidden? Is he afraid of us? . . . the people cried out laughingly.

The madman continues his perceptive ravings about the death and the funeral of God but comes to his own conclusion: " I

am come too early. I am not yet at the right time. This pro-
digious event is still on its way — it has not yet reached men's
ears."[16] The fanatic who loses his audience because he is light-
years ahead of them is similar to the one who does so because
he is light-years behind them. The *mythos* of the mature and
secularized world in which God is dead is as removed into the
mists of a future as the *mythos* of the religious world in which
God still lived, acted, spoke, and in which his voice was a
summons for belief is removed into the past. And when a
prophet enters the picture with denunciations based on a context that the modern community does not even remotely share
or with a cheap grace that the modern community is not even
seeking, his mask too is not believable and the self is not actually presented with the voice.

Without wanting to imply that the attempts at communicating frontally through mass media that were chronicled in the
previous chapter were in any way fanatic, I would suggest that
they come under this scope. Indeed, they are frequently so
routinized, so reduced to formula, or engaged in with such
an apathetic sense of ritual and role that they are dismissed:
the earthen vessel crumbles because it does not care about
holding the sacred treasure. The self and the mask are not
perceivable or believable because they do not take the voice
with its foundation-shaking possibility seriously. Despite the
gentility and smoothness of production, we are dealing with a
content that implies an ecstasy turned sour, a revelatory break-
through that has hardened into a routinized fanaticism.

To understand how easily the nonreligious or the religious
audience dismisses the head-on and virtually maskless proclamation, we must observe one whom they would regard as
fanatic. Anyone who has studied a crowd listening to a street-
corner preacher of pathological bent, be it at Broadway and
Forty-second or State and Madison or Hollywood and Vine,
has seen the problem vivified. Let us reconstruct a typical message, and see the problem. Picture a bearded, banner-waving,
deep-set-eyed prophet who has begun shouting and has

gathered an audience to whom he is soon going to hand out
tracts entitled "Are You Washed in the Blood of the Lamb?"
Were we to make a tape-recording, it could come out something like this:

"Men and brethren, gather round. Men and brethren, sinners all, you don't have much time. The glass of history, the
hourglass, is running out. You don't have much time. And you
had plenty of time. You pleasure-lovers, you tavern-goers, you
lusters and Mammon-seekers, your time is running out. Men
and brethren, you had time ever since Eve gave Adam the
apple, and he did eat thereof. And you wouldn't believe when
Noah made the ark, and you had one hundred and twenty-five
years. And Jonah came to this town, yes, sir, he came to
Nineveh and your time is running out, he said, after he got out
of the fish. It was not a whale but a big fish, and there are still
big fish. And you wouldn't listen, so your time is running out.
But the same Lord up in heaven who flares his nostrils at the
pleasure-loving, tavern-going, lusting, Mammon-seeking lot of
you also sent his Lamb to give his blood for you. He poured it
out for you, but the time is running short and it is dripping
away. But the Lamb came and John saw his blood and shouted,
'Behold the Lamb of God that takes away the sin of the whole
world!' His name is Je-a-sus, and God talked about him in
the Garden, and this is he about whom Noah and Jonah and
the fish were prophesying.

"And Jesus went to people like you whose time was running
out. He went to the pleasure-lovers, the tavern-goers; he went
to Mary Magdalene and the little man Zacchaeus up the tree
and he talked to them. He raised dead people up from the dead
and when they had leprosy he cured them. And the Lamb came
to pour out a fountain of blood, and he did when they killed
him and pierced him. And this Lamb — and your time is running out and the blood is flowing past you and drying — was
raised from the dead. He's coming! He's coming! He'll come
back and burn you in hell if you keep on lusting for women
and money. He has the power. Lucifer was defeated and

Je-a-sus the Lamb has power to roast you, and his blood is still flowing.

"But he is the King and he poured out that blood for you and if you read this little page I'm passing out — no charge at all, of course — you will know that his blood will wash you and like the hyssop will make you whiter than snow. But you have to turn and surrender and accept the Lamb. You have to have the baptizing of fire that my words give you and you have to leave the cocktail taverns and the Mammon and you have to have the Spirit."

The printed page hardly helps recapture the grotesqueness of the street-corner prophet of Christianity. This sermonette is taken from notes I made in New York in 1958; it is edited, but no doubt no more so than are the sermons in the book of The Acts. Some of the illustrative material was deleted for brevity's sake and the rhetorical sense cannot be reproduced. But the outline is accurate.

Anyone who has heard such a sermon in such a setting knows the nature of the reaction. The minstreling prophet may have with him a little coterie of believers to pass out the tracts, to build up faith, to lead the cheering cheering-section. But ordinarily he is a "loner," alienated, representing only himself. The crowd is curious, but not so curious as to what is in it for them as it is for the study of the pathological personality or the rhetorical ring. Some will bait and lead him on, others will pass knowing smiles. Most people will be a bit embarrassed and pass by on the other side. No one will identify, no one accepts, the voice as a summons for belief. The self presented so frontally is not a believable self. The message is neglected or rejected. But the message itself should not be rejected by that mass, for certainly a large minority actually, given the chance to demythologize a bit, already believes it. The majority that rejects at least explores the option when it appears in other forms or versions. Notice its parallel to the summary of apostolic preaching prepared by Archibald M. Hunter:

A reporter's summary of an early Christian sermon would have read something like this:

The prophecies are fulfilled, and the New Age has dawned.
The Messiah, born of David's seed, has appeared.
He is Jesus of Nazareth, God's Servant, who
    Went about doing good and healing by God's power,
    Was crucified according to God's purpose,
    Was raised from the dead on the third day,
    Is now exalted to God's right hand,
    And will come again in glory for judgment.
Therefore let all repent and believe and be baptized for the forgiveness of sins and the gift of the Holy Spirit.[17]

What our street-corner preacher is doing, then, is reproducing *largely in Biblical language* the *kērygma,* or New Testament proclamation. Without denying the legitimacy of a proclamation of this sort or the sects or cults that it produces in and around the Christian church, I do not think we need labor this point: that the proclamation can be presented in unbelievable forms even in its frontality. The person behind the mask may not always be believable, and the presentation of Christ, his people, and the Christian self may misplace the scandal, may offend in the wrong way for the wrong reason.

If we polish the edges of the person and render genteel and gentle the nature of the proclamation, it is still possible that the content as presented will *unnecessarily* lose the audience in mass communications. The intention may be admirable, the person sincere, the manner forthright, yet all is lost. It is a case, to borrow Reinhold Niebuhr's terms, of presenting a messiah where no messiah is expected. It uses the language of a *mythos* that is no longer new but seems to have been tried and found wanting and cannot be reinvested with meaning. It misplaces the offense of God's revelation and freezes its meaning by identification with certain formulas ("Are you washed in the blood of the Lamb?"). It may be true in that it could promote belief *that,* but it cannot be believable in the sense of generating belief *in*. It is this form of Christian use of mass media exclusively that came under criticism previously.

Does this mean that the proclamation is not to be offered in the twentieth century? Must we, like Nietzsche's madman, intone a requiem at the burial of the God of the proclamation? Not at all. The mighty acts of God do not change, and his voice still summons. The proclamation makes sense to the Christian community or the expectant community. But mass media are addressed to those who have already dismissed the Christian option partly because its context seemed meaningless.

We have been dealing, then, with only one of at least three possible means of approach. There is proclamatory presentation on mass media. In the nonreligious sense, it is believable even in the crass sense of commercial messages. Something new is offered to people who are expecting it: the novelty of soaps with built-in cold cream, unfailing television antennae for one dollar, toothpaste with stripes of mouthwash: these are the messianic hopes of a wrinkly-skinned, fading-pictured, offending-breathed era. The announcer proclaims, and the people buy. The demagogue shouts, and when the soil is fertile, the seed grows. For the proclamation meets existing expectations, fills men's hopes with proper opinions and useful products.

In the religious sense, there is also a believable use of proclamation. Christianity offers meaning ("Though he slay me, yet will I trust in him") and is dismissed by an age in quest of substance. Religion offers substance. Belief in God produces peace of mind. This makes people like you better, and this produces prosperity. We can rewrite Archibald Hunter's summary of the *kērygma* in religious terms:

> You have been told that things would get better as life went on. That possibility is now here. Belief in God and in yourself is the key, and that possibility is yours if you only want it, and if you learn how not to worry.
> Have faith in the power of a positive idea and a selfless action. Go about doing good.
> This faith and activity will pay off. Doctors today know much

about psychosomatic medicine. They know that if our minds and spirits are healthy, our bodies will be healthy. So faith will be useful in giving you a happier and longer life. You may have to make some sacrifices toward the goal. But these are only a temporary setback, and you will soon be raised to new possibilities.

You know people suffer — either now or later — for their negative thoughts, their projection of evil to others, their failure to have faith. You can escape this suffering. The possibility is yours.

So change your mind and decide to use the spiritual resources that are yours. And things will get better: you will make more money, have new friends, and most of all — inner peace.

All this is proclamation. It is not easily validated. But it fills the expectations and forms the proper opinions for an age in quest of easy assurance and comfortable moralism. Again, the context matters. The self presented behind the voice is believable.

The Christian *kērygma* in a nonreligious or religious world suffers from the fact that it has been tried and already dismissed. To the faithful gathered on a Sunday morning, its possibility is there. To the existentialist, the especially perceptive person, the individual with neurotic anxiety, its option still has transforming power. But the casual, prosperous, and unquestioning " unknown citizen " does not permit the interruption of his life by the proclamation, whether by street-corner evangelist or in other forms.

A decisive illustration of this difficulty in relation to the central Christian proclamation comes from contemporary literature. It is implied in the title of an article by Amos N. Wilder, " The Cross: Social Trauma or Redemption."[18]

I do not think it is possible to present the Christian faith without the cross of Jesus Christ. This is the center of its scandal of particularity; this is the historic moment on which the whole drama of redemption — for its time or forever — turns. Wilder would agree. But he asks whether the concept of the meaning of suffering has not significantly changed, making the meaning of the cross as much a part of pathology or gibberish as it seemed to be in the mouth of the street-corner preacher.

Wilder sees the reason at the heart of today's dismissal as inhering in the picture today's poet or novelist renders of Jesus, based on today's questions and misconceptions. "The saving death and resurrection have been fitted into a slot in this or that schema of redeemer-archetypes provided by cultural studies in myth and ritual, and so evacuated of any distinctive significance." The terminology of seasonal fertility rites and the symbols of Gnostic regeneration color the New Testament account in the mind of the informed layman. He does not recognize the decisive difference between faith based on revelation through historical experience and religion based on nature or on nature and the soul.

The intellectual merely sophisticates what the passers-by on the New York street are doing. He dismisses Christ because he must dismiss morbid forms of Christianity as they are presented en masse. Wilder's example is *Dear Judas*, by Robinson Jeffers, which emphasizes suffering as the clue to the appeal of Christianity. This misconception is the fault of Christians: "They have all too easily identified the cross or the blood of Christ with mere suffering or let this motif play too large a part." The faith looks like sadism or masochism and is then properly annihilated as subhuman or antipersonal. Sub-Christian asceticism, self-punishment, or orgiastic religious exercises have nurtured this picture. The metaphor of the street-corner evangelist and many a Christian frontalist in mass media communication adds to the complication. Fundamentalists used to write off as modernists all who were not at home with the "blood" motif. But it is possible to keep the scandal of Christianity and still to recognize the complex character of pictures derived from animal sacrifice, a meaningless ritual today.

Now what we have here is a very fundamental issue. There are not a few modern intellectuals who genuinely believe that Christianity, centering as it does in the cross, has exerted its power by an appeal to, and indeed a secret stimulus to, man's hidden obsession with suffering and even blood lust. . . .It is not surprising that such observers find it difficult to draw the line between the healthy and the morbid.

For George Bernard Shaw, the crucifixion "became to the churches what the chamber of horrors is to a waxwork: the irresistible attraction for children and for the crudest adult worshipers."

Wilder's comment is apropos the difficulty proclamatory preaching has on mass media if the mass and not the Christian community is implied:

> The theologian is confronted in all such views with a major challenge. The scandal of the cross is sharp enough without adding to it this unnecessary element. But there are undoubtedly many discerning men and women who misunderstand the Christian faith just at this point. They find it tainted with morbidity and they are abetted in their error by widely current Christian attitudes and practices. . . . But the theologian can also make clear that there is no proper foothold in the Christian story for man's persistent and recurrent morbidity, his impulse to give pain or to endure pain, his propensity for mortification and maceration.

The excrescences of Christian piety that are often associated with the proclamation of Christ crucified can be dismissed within the Christian community, for there the over-all purpose is seen. But to the society that has rejected the context or the *mythos,* this is a greater hazard. For it, different forms must be found. And Wilder is again a help here. The Passion of Christ ended on Good Friday. The risen and triumphant Christ shares in the continuing struggle of the church militant and the martyrs. The deeper sense of this is that God is not impassible but is "afflicted with all our afflictions." He participates and calls his children to participate in the world's existence — even when that includes suffering.

The difference lies between morbid suffering and meaningful suffering. *It is the context of the Christian community that makes the distinction possible,* that clothes with joy the nakedness and unnecessary additions to the offense of the proclamation. For it is a body of representative persons, often healthy and happy, who can say individually, " Now I rejoice in my sufferings for your sake, and in my flesh I complete what is lacking in Christ's afflictions for the sake of his body, that is, the church " (Col. 1:24).

To return to Wilder:

> The secret of the suffering of the Christian, according to the New Testament, is that this suffering is indissolubly merged with joy: " suffering but always rejoicing," what Luther called *Kreuzseligkeit*. To leave this out is to fall back into heathenism and into the " sorrow of the world " which " worketh death." " For as we share abundantly in Christ's sufferings, so through Christ we share abundantly in comfort too."

The cross of Christ should be a fountain of health and not of morbidity. The Gospels are austere; they do not dwell on the morbid. Christian proclamation over mass media, when it is merely frontal and does not participate in the context of the hearer, lapses into heathenism — and today's good pagan recognizes it or is unnecessarily rejected by religious man who does not see that Christian self-giving is purposeful.

Thus the novel that devotes itself to the *kērygma* is easily dismissed as tractarian or propagandistic. It loses its art and its market. It neither gains the whole world nor keeps its Christian soul. The magazine article that divorces itself from context makes Christianity seem to be a curiosity, a survival. Newspaper advertisements about " the blood of the Lamb " mean no more to the urbane reader than do patent-medicine advertisements. Movies that proclaim through the morbid (the leprosy of *Ben-Hur* in its " Revised Standard Version " of 1959 comes to mind) fascinate but do not compel one to entertain the Christian option. Shouting evangelists on radio actually tend to build walls against the faith. As for television, the same would hold true. There must be a more excellent way, yet one consistent with true Christianity.

I believe there are many ways, but they can be clustered around two ideas. The frontal, proclamatory approach that is so effective within the Christian community is the *kērygma;* the other forms are *didachē* and *marturia, leitourgia, diakonia:* "witness," "service," "Christian activity." *Kērygma* is fully explicit and direct; the third complex is a largely implicit and indirect witness; *didachē* is borderline, permitting elaboration.

Didachē

Although a legitimate goal of Christian work through mass media is to bring people into the context of community in which proclamation is effective, this does not make other forms of witness unimportant. It may be true, as C. H. Dodd has written, that "while the church was concerned to hand on the teaching of the Lord, it was not by this that it made converts. It was by *kērygma,* says Paul, not by *didachē,* that it pleased God to save man."[19]

But when the presentation of Christ or his people occurs through the mask of the media a different situation comes into existence. Now the chance to elaborate on the mysteries provides the Christian with new opportunities. This elaboration is an extremely important task in religiously illiterate America.

The absence of the imaginatively didactic element in the public presentation of Christianity has added to the offense. The faith can be dismissed without a hearing because Americans feel that they already know what it has to say. A culture like our own, shaped as it is in no small part by Protestantism, so identifies itself with that faith as culture but not as revelation that it expects no surprises. Yet the substance, the content, the promise of the faith, receives no hearing. In part, this is the result of a mass culture that has provided so many distractions. In part it is the product of American anti-intellectualism, though this charge might easily be overdone. In part it is the fault of the churches, which, in their stress on the warm heart and on practical piety, have left behind considerations of the content of the faith.

Thus although proclamation provides the opportunity for Christ himself to be presented (as the paradox, the Improper Opinion, for belief *in*), Christianity also has room for elaborative witness, the knowledge that builds up and edifies the Christian and the church. The basic cast of American religions has been Arminian, no matter what their names. There has always been a sort of healthy activism and optimism, a practical interest in good works that — when associated with the Christian fullness — strikes an authentic note. But the branch of piety and works grew, and the stem and root of faith and knowledge withered; no one had tended it.

Every survey of religious literacy (whether this has to do with what might be called saving knowledge or with interesting information) is consistent in its depressing report. Even so primitive a matter as the naming of the first four books of the New Testament causes dismay (and further documents the problem of the Book, so widely purchased and so little read). As recently as 1950 the Gallup poll quizzed Americans about this point. Allowing for as much inaccuracy as we will, the summary still should alarm the Christian who thinks that faith is propagated through the witness to Christ in the Gospels.

Fifty-three per cent of the American people on this projection could not name *any* of the four Gospels. Four per cent named one; 4 per cent, two; 4 per cent, three; and 35 per cent named all four correctly. (A British survey found 61 per cent able to name all four.) In America the illiteracy became more serious with youth, a fact counter to trends in general literacy. Only 26 per cent between the ages of 21 and 29 named all four Gospels; 36 per cent in the 30- to 49-age bracket could do it; 39 per cent of the over 50's could. Of course, the ability to name the Gospels has very little to do directly with the quality of our faith, but it points to an abysmal lack of awareness of the sources of the faith's content and witness.

In such a world, Christianity then comes not as a familiar

friend who provides coziness and security but as a disturbing stranger who should have something really new to offer. We know little of some religions because we are too remote from them; we know little of Christianity because we are so close. We stand near it and see only a fragment. We judge the Kingdom of God by the quality of the bake sale at the Main Street Church or the personality of a minister we once knew or the cost of an edifice to which we once contributed.

However, if the mystery of the Christian faith, the tantalizing character of its promise, were portrayed, we should again hold the interest of a representative part of the mass audience. The content of the teaching is the same as of the preaching, though it may include many elements not needed in proclamation. Teaching is not dishonored in the New Testament. The disciples devoted themselves to it after Pentecost (Acts 2:42) just as Jesus spent most of his ministry training them, preparing to send them out as sheep among wolves. There was place for the substance of things hoped for, the doctrine, the wisdom, the knowledge, even the information: the truths about the Truth.

It has been pointed out that only one of the New Testament lists of vocations that have been granted the one Spirit for the diversity of tasks includes the evangelist (Eph. 4:11, in contrast to Rom. 12:6–8; I Cor. 12:8–10, 28–30). The early church recognized that faith was built up not only by reflections upon the activity of God in history and on the events of the life of Jesus (which play almost no part in the Pauline corpus) but also by correlating the decisive event — the sacrifice and service on the cross — to the cosmic purpose and to the human disciplines of thought.

Perhaps it sounds strange to suggest that this correlating can and should be done today through mass media when people approach them largely for escape or casually. That Christian teaching can be deadeningly dull scarcely needs to be documented. Should the opportunity be presented the church today to say something informative, we might be embarrassed

by how unprepared we are, either methodologically or in the
matter of content. And that people show an almost invincible
ignorance or a virtually cosmic indifference to most teaching
that goes on is equally apparent.

To stress teaching, further, is not to make an intellectualistic
or Gnostic assumption. Christianity is not to be classified with
the mystery religions that seek their cult for initiation and the
extension of divine power through esoteric information. It is
not a faith reserved for the rationally proud or the intellectually
mighty: God chose the foolish things, says Paul, to confound
the wise. It is true that, in my accent on teaching as a borderline opportunity between true but impotent proclamation and
powerful but substantially limited portrayal of service, it may
appear that I must rely on those occasionally optimistic break-
throughs on mass media.

None of these assumptions need be true. When people are
shown something that confronts them in the context of the life
which they now live, yet which represents a voice from beyond
summoning for belief, they will give at least more than a passing ear to hearing " What is in it for me." Their interest may be
motivated by selfish or religious concerns, but it provides the
soil in which Christian seed can be sown, the seed that like the
grain of wheat dies to live. Teaching need not be done in a
formal, condescending manner. It, too, may be most effective
when informal, indirect, implicit.

Energy invested in the endeavor is particularly worth-while
in an age when religion finds favor and when Christianity must
gain its effect by first separating itself a few feet from its environment. One of the problems of Christianity in its religious
environment is this: we can assume the good will of the
American people; but this good will serves immediately to
translate and to domesticate the Christian demand or gift. The
love that is engendered by faith needs more arts than rhetoric
to keep it warm. It would not be possible to document this
guess: probably more Christian action today proceeds from
sermons to which people respond by saying, " I never knew

that before " than from sermons on which they comment, " My, that was an inspiring sermon! " This is true particularly if the *that* refers to something in the revealing plan of God and not just to the dust on the Dead Sea scrolls or a *logion* from an Egyptian gospel, however helpful the latter may be for gaining interest and for novelty.

If what I am saying is true, we are in a situation somewhat contrary to that of the New Testament when we imply mass media. Then *kērygma* was for the outside world, *didachē* for building up the faithful. Mass communications can spread proclamation so haphazardly broadcast that it is meaningless, but it can use the teaching as a promissory note, a preliminary mask for the presentation of Christianity's larger self.

The forms for such teaching are manifold, and we may illustrate some. A novel of some competence, *The Devil's Advocate,* by Morris West, made its way to a spot sufficiently high on the best-seller lists to be considered a mass medium of expression. It was an entertaining book in its own right; the story was competent. But more, it revealed in graphic terms the apparent ambiguity in Roman Catholic teaching that has been a puzzlement to outsiders and an embarrassment to many within. It showed how the possibility of sainthood could be envisioned in relation to an obvious and almost open sinner. John Howard Griffin's novel, *The Devil Rides Outside,* in its exploration of the sinning outsider in the monastic community was similar; and this has been an enduring theme in the work of Graham Greene.

In magazines Christians have frequently been given the opportunity to teach. Sometimes the possibility exists because the ground rules of American debate allow for several options including the religious and the Christian. In such a setting the Christian need not be a concessionist; he can be forthright in presenting the option. Popular magazines tend to focus on the more public issues: church and state, birth control, divorce; or on the more promising personal answers: anxiety, guilt, faith, mental health. But in any of these the opportunity to attract people by presenting the teaching mask of the church is apparent. One example that comes to mind instantly is the noteworthy series by Leo Rosten in *Look* magazine, 1952 to 1955, in which representatives of various faiths answered questions that dealt with the nature of the hope that was in them. The total effect, of course, is dimmed by the fact of pluralism, by the competing textures and the varying claims. But this is less the fault of the magazine, its editor, the people interviewed, and the readership than it is in the way the cards of history are dealt in a pluralistic society and in the sinful divisiveness of Christianity, historically and in its present actuality.

Sometimes newspapers provide the opportunity for teaching. Often they are more fascinated by the esoteric or the irregular. Father Divine, Daddy Grace, and the eccentric tradition are often given more space than historic Christianity. But again and again in picture and print newspapers may offer meaningful asides on the mysteries of the faith as explained to them by the men who make stained glass or design churches or minister in slums.

Motion pictures provide the least opportunity for this form of presentation. The didactic element is least at home in dramatic arts; when the teaching becomes explicit, the art is lost. The expense of production, the captivity of the audience that has paid the price of the ticket and is not now in position to select what is offered, the sense of fairness — all these tend to prevent expansion on the faith's mysteries and the extent of God's revelation.

Radio provides more opportunities because, as a nonvisual form, it must rely to a large extent on voice and the presentation of ideas. So the discussion show on radio and television has opened up new possibilities. I am not deceived: such programs are not the most popular and they reach limited audiences. But depth interviews and televised panel programs of discussion have made a decisive impact on the American listening and viewing audience, and the possibility should not be underestimated. Often we have heard Christian teaching of a profound nature winsomely presented on such programs. However, ordinarily the conversation programs find their justification in discussion of public issues — this is understandable — and the groundwork is often implied. Nevertheless, articulate representatives of the faith often are given the chance to describe the promise of that faith, and more attention could be given to this use of the media.

The advantages of this approach are obvious. The nonreligious person cannot lightly dismiss teaching of a profound character, even when it is necessarily simply stated. For he knows that such teaching leads to his self-understanding. With Paul Tillich he senses even if he does not know that religion is the soul of his culture and culture the form of religion. Even if he lives in a self-consciously post-Christian society and if the assumptions of Christendom are slipping away, he knows that enough of Christianity remains as a substructure that he must become familiar with it in order to know who he is, what his past is, and what his hopes are. He also knows that Christianity is one of the live options in a pluralistic society; and even if he has bypassed it or outgrown it, there it remains as an enduring possibility.

The religious person may at first be embarrassed by Christian teaching, for in our society religiousness has taken on the colors of the dominant faith, Christianity. It may disturb him to see how far removed are Christian claims from his own securities. He will find out for the first time how much distance there is between his moralism and Christianity's annihilating law and healing grace. He will see many securities and complacencies removed. He will see how late in the moral quest he is to exhaust his response to God's total demand on him, and how suddenly and sweetly grace will then be recognized. But even if in original fury and permanent embarrassment he listens, listen he will if the talk is about him.

For comparison, notice the popularity attained by the books that taught Americans about their place in life. During the 1950's, numbers of books criticizing the culture, because they were best sellers — *The Waist-High Culture, The House of Intellect, The Lonely Crowd, The Status Seekers, The Organization Man* — became the manuals of the people they set out to criticize. Part of their appeal was no doubt narcissistic. Seldom did reading of the books issue in different kinds of action. But each provided the self-understanding necessary for developing a more organic view of life. In religion, books like Will Herberg's *Protestant — Catholic — Jew*, a scathing indictment of belongingness in American religion, at least indirectly reached and affected large masses of people. It involved a great deal of *didachē* of the highest order: the kind that leads to self-understanding and cultural criticism with an aim toward betterment. The religious reader of the book, unless he built insulation against its claim, must have been inspired to explore the particularities of the faiths there described.

The possibilities of teaching for the Christian element in the mass audience are multiple and attractive. Remember, for example, that the Gallup poll found the low level of knowledge of Christianity's basic witness to the Lord in 53 per cent of the American people at a moment when scarcely 40 per cent of the American people were not affiliated with organized religious groups. Christian action would be significantly magnified if its people, responding to a magazine article or a television panel, could say, " I never knew *that* before," and were prompted to desire to put the *that* into their lives.

Here as elsewhere there are dangers. The danger of selecting elements that will entertain and fascinate are apparent. It is the preoccupation with novelty in teaching that makes the Saturday-afternoon advertisements of Sunday sermon titles so ludicrous. Each week it is possible to guess the subject of these " didactic " sermons. In February they will relate Lincoln's religion to the Christian faith. While her spirit hovered in the headlines the Christian community had to be regaled with accounts of Bridey Murphy and the Christian faith. When there are television scandals the contrast between Charles Van Doren and Christian morality can be drawn out in ten thousand pulpits and a thousand radio broadcasts. All the temptations to men in the pulpit to make themselves cultically current are magnified by the men in the mass media. Much as we may satirize the point of origination of these discussions, they do provide springboards for authentic Christian witness.

In late 1959 and early 1960, for instance, there was a good deal of interest in the subject of birth control. It was occasioned almost entirely by mass media. A television program was devoted to the "population explosion." The Catholic bishops studied a report to the President by the Draper Committee and brought the controversy into the open. Bishop James Pike, working in no small measure through space in the Luce magazines, challenged Roman Catholic candidates for office to declare themselves.

Instantly the subject was on everyone's lips. Obviously it had sensational overtones and some often ugly political undertones. But follow-through made possible the intelligent discussion by Roman Catholics and Protestants of certain Christian teachings of a basic character. In the best of these discussions, the stewardship and use of the earth, the doctrine of Creation and the responsibility for procreation, and the subject of natural law always came to the front and center as challenges and options for all readers and hearers.

Another instance of the way mass media of communications assist in Christian teaching, even if obliquely from the viewpoint of some Christian groups: For fifty years the ecumenical movement had been taking on form. It was visible and tangible. *Within* the church it was the great new fact of our era. Separated Christians took hope from the vision it brought. But every representative of the movement was forewarned that the term "ecumenical" could not possibly be communicated to any but those sufficiently well equipped intellectually or theologically. Even to mention it would alienate an audience that was shaped by media that would not tolerate anything so "egghead" as a Greek word for a modern spiritual reality.

For a long time we believed this to be true; self-consciously the term must be avoided or patronizingly set off in quotation marks. Then one morning the wire services carried the story that Pope John XXIII had called for an ecumenical council. Because of mass media, riders of the subway and clerks at their counters all knew by the end of the morning rush hour what the call word meant. The discussion that ensued showed that the call and its dissemination had been overstated both by the Pontiff and the mass media, but the media then provided opportunity for quieter discussion of a subject that is also near the world's heart. And ecumenicity became not only the private property of the church's learned but the opportunity for the church to reveal its hope to the world. A central Christian teaching was exposed to the public because of mass media and through them. *Didachē* has only begun to be explored as a form of communication in a complex world.

Christian Activity: Marturia, Leitourgia, Diakonia

If proclamation loses its audience and teaching bores it (at their worst), a third form of the mask for presenting Christ and his people never fails to attract. No single word covers this mask well. I once heard a professor of missions say that the best form of apologetics for the mission front could be summarized in the two slang sentences: "This is what makes us tick. Give it a whirl." "This" . . . "it" refer to the proclamation and the teaching. "Making us tick" refers to a different complex and test for the faith. It applies to the indirect method of pointing to Christ by pointing to his church. It refers to the presentation of the church's self through the lives of its people as masks. Mass media are most effective when dealing with this form.

We have signaled parts of this complex by reference to several Greek words. The first of these is *marturia*, "testimony" or "testifying." It refers to the activity of those who have seen the Lord, including those of later generations who are contemporary with him, directly in some senses and indirectly in the work of his church. " That which was from the beginning, which we have heard, which we have seen with our eyes, which we have looked upon and touched with our hands concerning the word of life — . . . we proclaim also to you, so that you may have fellowship with us." (I John 1:1, 3.) Here is not only witness by proclaiming and by reference to " that which was " but also to the persistent " we." The church would win the world by pointing to itself.

At first glance this seems particularly hazardous. Christ is safely remote in history; his offense can be glossed over by the silk of a Hollywood beard or the pink clothes of a magazine illustration. But the edge of the church is exposed in the world. Its own temptations to power, its own faintheartedness, its own pride and lovelessness, are too apparent for it to attract either a righteous nonreligious world or a morally secure religious one. But unless we are Monophysites and if we want to do justice to God's drenching of himself in human history, we must live with this hazard and let it be exposed. Both in the suffering and in the joy of Christian persons there is room for Christian witness of a contemporary character.

Leitourgia is a second element in the complex of Christian activity. It refers to service, but only in part that of a cultic kind. Paul speaks of being " poured as a libation upon the sacrificial offering of your faith " (Phil. 2:17). Frequently, *leitourgia* refers to the routine activity of servants of the church. The portrayal of Christians going about their activity of presenting themselves as living sacrifices to God is an effective part of their presentation of themselves to the world. *Diakonia* also means service, in this case often with a more menial (but no less compelling) connotation. The service of preparing a meal, the office of the prophets and the apostles, the aid, support, and charitable work in which they engage — all these are part of Christian activity.

The same hazards are apparent in all these activities. A church that is irreverent and selfish, that does not render itself to God in worship and commend itself to men through service, will cancel the good promissory and preliminary impression it makes through mass media. Activity and promise must be at least relatively parallel. But even in its failure the church shows here an attractive side, for in its activity it is identifying with the world that God created, in which he was incarnate and in which the redemptive drama was enacted.

When we turn to mass media we could say the form of presentation here implied is simply the reporting of events and news. The compelling power of a story is never to be underestimated. Christianity has always made its way as a good story, well reported. An account of the acts of God in the lives of men can insinuate itself into the consciousness of people in ways that proclamation and teaching cannot. Its effects may be more memorable and more profound even though it cannot be self-sufficient, cannot stand alone; it must also have verbal presentation with clarity of outline. Whether in the part of the dialectic that sees Christianity identifying with the larger community or in that part which sees it withdrawn, the life of Christ in his people still wins attention.

It is not immoral or contrary to Christian virtues for the church to want to commend itself to men. It is commanded to make such a presentation. And here mass media of communication can be of great help as masks of this revelation. For they allow, as Erving Goffman reminded us that all self-conscious role-playing does, for a certain theatricalization of the common rhythms of life. A certain selectivity is here involved. Although the picture that the church presents of itself must be honest and must be consistent with the reality, by the very nature of the media it will be clear that the decisive moments, the *kairoi*, will be reported on. All life allows for a certain waste, a certain almost monotonous but still healthy sequence of nonsignificant moments. They are soon swallowed by oblivion. But the crises, the real turns in the road — these are captured for memory.

So with Christian history and the lives within the church to-day. Ever since the writers of the Gospels, Christians have honored the biographers, the witnesses to the lives of others moved by God. More people have been compelled to the Christian faith by the example of a Saint Francis or a William Wilberforce than by anything these saints ever said or wrote. " Here is what makes them tick. Give it a whirl." Although we receive our extension of the meaning of the Christ-event from the epistolary literature, it is the story in the Gospels and the book of The Acts that is vivid in our minds from childhood.

At this point all the media offer examples. Of books chronicling the fact and fiction of common Christian sainthood, there is no limit. Newspapers are less reluctant to call attention to Christianity through the news it makes than because of the words it says. Of course, one cannot simply decide to make news. One cannot contrive Christian action and do this as an attention-getting device. The safeguards are twofold: Christianity itself does not permit this approach to " what the Gentiles seek " as a permanent strategy, and the world soon spots the phoniness of institutions avowedly spiritual when they set the wrong goals.

But the church is often in the news, and when it is thrust there — this is all to the better. The more the church acts like the church, the more newsworthy it will be. All the propaganda and programs can then be displaced. As an example: when an ugly racial situation breaks out in the North or the South, the chances are that if a creative minority begins to appear, it will — unless it has been latent in a quiet but organized pressure group — first of all erupt in churches and sometimes among the clergy in particular. When nothing happens to protest injustice, the world makes known its disgust with the church. When something happens and the church is willing to risk unpopularity in its local community, the world watches. Even where the world does not share the courage — or even the idea — it is tantalized by a spirit and a force that after so many centuries burns anew in the lives of people who " go about doing good."

When the issue at hand is particularly unpopular the church may for a time be considered so completely out of step that it is shrugged off. People who on Christian principles warn against nuclear fallout and atomic armaments are often dismissed as " oddballs," and apparently their efforts, though they make news, are of no avail. As often as not, the Spirit guards his impulses, however, and the long pull of events gives some assurance that authentic suffering and service by the church in the world win the apathetic to a vision that is longed for and that will not be dimmed. The fact that communism makes more headlines now than does the vision it would dull is to be accounted for not only by the movement as a demonic power but also is a tribute to the idea and the view of history it has generated in an hour of Christian failure of nerve or indifference.

Motion pictures provide numbers of examples. Perhaps the finest religious motion picture yet produced was the French film *Monsieur Vincent*, the life of Vincent de Paul. With an absolute minimum of proclamation and with little interest in teaching, it was the mask for presenting the aspiration of the whole church through the noiseless portrayal of the life of an accessible and modern saint among miserable people. In such artistic hands the film has possibilities that are seldom realized.

As concerns radio, its situation is similar to that of the newspaper. Television is again in many ways unique because of its system of sponsorship. In its more public presentations one can be Christian if he is not too Christian, and thus the result is often a sort of generalized (quasi-Jewish) Biblical faith or mere religiousness. What the producers of the great movie *Ben-Hur* achieved is the goal — understandably — of television producers: when the faith is presented, make it attractive to the Christian majority without making it unattractive to the Jewish or secular minorities. But for all the risks of diminution and muffling through the mask of drama, the portrayal without much verbalization and without any explicit proclamation of the power of God in human lives seems to be the only way of seeing the faith at " prime time " where it really reaches masses.

The impact of the portrayal of Christian action can be measured again in the various audiences that make up a mass society. The immediate response of the nonreligious viewer is skepticism or wistfulness: skepticism because people do not *act* that way, or at least the portrayal will not seem fully consistent with the Christianity he sees on Main Street; wistfulness because it suggests an impulse he does not share. But the long-run effect of Christian activity is to woo and to win when action as summons for belief is consistent with the voice and the Word.

The religious reader or member of an audience will be unsettled, for *marturia, leitourgia,* and *diakonia* proceed from motives he does not understand through paths he is not sure he wants to follow. That Christians often presuppose a religious audience is clear from a bulletin put out some years ago by the Protestant Council of New York City as reproduced by William H. Whyte and later repudiated by the Council. It told " speakers on its radio and television programs ":

> Subject matter should project love, joy, courage, hope, faith, trust in God, good will. Generally avoid condemnation, criticism, controversy. In a very real sense we are "selling " religion, the good news of the gospel. Therefore admonitions and training of Christians on cross-bearing, forsaking all else, sacrifices, and service usually cause the average listener to turn the dial. Consoling the bereaved and calling sinners to repentance, by direct indictment of the listeners is out of place (with designated exceptions). . . .
> As apostles, can we not extend an invitation, in effect: " Come and enjoy our privileges, meet good friends, see what God can do for you! "[20]

Admittedly, this advice shows some insight into the mass audience. It implies — and properly so — that dreariness should not be associated with the faith; it recognizes the serious limits of denunciatory proclamation to a community that does not share the judgmental context. But what about " cross-bearing, forsaking all else, sacrifices, and service," which causes dial-turning?

Here we face a dilemma that the first two forms of presentation, proclamation or teaching, do little to solve. Shall one lose the audience or does he cater to the supposed wants of the majority and let his appeal degenerate into religiousness? I submit that the only solution comes not from talking about sacrifice and service but rather by portraying lives and events in which their invitatory power is revealed. The question is as much one of tactic as of theology. Theologically the problem is this: Will one ever learn discipleship if the first confrontation is on other terms? Jesus' approach was precisely the opposite. However winningly he might work, always a sense of the full implication of discipleship was recklessly thrown at the prospect. Somehow Jesus always knew at what to pull in a man's system of security, what it was that would permanently prevent real discipleship were it not countered from the first. To the rich young ruler (Matt. 19:16–22) whom he would win from his religious security and sense of moral superiority he works on possession; to others, on vocation or family. Mark adds of the young man, " and Jesus looking upon him loved him," but he risked " turning the dial " for the sake of the value of discipleship.

Finally, the Christian element in a readership or an audience should respond. For the call to discipleship and service is never an abstraction or a general principle. It is always the concrete " Follow me," without plans laid out for the respondent. And hearing of, reading about, or seeing the concrete call as it is worked out in other lives illumines our own.

The process, then, works something like this: one is, presumably, tantalized by a portrayal of the Christian life in all its complexity and ambiguity but with some sense of the joyful sacrifice and serenity of forgiveness that is a part of that life. Such a presentation is a mask, in a sense a performance, though it must be consistent with the self that projects it. There is no evasion of the scandal of the cross; such an approach knows nothing except Christ crucified. But it knows this neither as a noisy slogan nor, to a lesser extent, as a complex of teachings, but rather as a participation on the part of God in man's life and, in exchange, a sharing of the divine life on the part of man. From this, one is drawn to a second stage where *didachē* is operative. Finally, if the follow-up is consistent and if local units are doing their work, there will come the chance to confront the man as an individual where he is and where the proclamation can best today be heard and understood, in the Christian community.

It is the voice that remains the summons for belief: but in *marturia, leitourgia, diakonia,* the voice is not only active through the mask of abstract personhood: the voice is made flesh, and its glory is beheld.

Chapter V

A Note on the Imagination:
A Protestant Problem

The problem of the presentation of the faith through mass media will be solved by Christians to the degree that they participate in this world's life successfully. They participate directly for the sake of identification yet, theologically, indirectly. For their relation to the world is always not as brother but as cousin once-removed through the Christ who reconciled the world unto God. When this dialectic is persistent and evident (however quietly it must occur by its very nature), it will become the subject of interest to creators of imaginative literature and drama as well as to newsmen.

Some years ago in an issue on mass communications, *Atlantic* printed a brilliant if cynical article, "What Makes News?"[21] by T. S. Matthews. First came the preliminaries:

Most of the news is manufactured through interviews, exaggerated reporting, press conferences, or informed speculation. Little of the news is really "what happened yesterday." A second way of making news is the tabloid's fashion: to ballyhoo unimportant features of personal lives. A third avenue of newsmaking is rumor, attention to small detail based on hearsay. Then comes attention to the basic problem. "The big good news is mainly manufactured, not so much because the press is sanguine by nature as because it is committed to the encouraging notion of progress." On the other hand, "the big bad news is what has actually happened":

Good news, in the public sense, is either incredible or beyond our understanding. And yet we crave it, its absence seems wrong, we want it to be. It's rather like the poem in which Thomas Hardy said that if someone asked him on Christmas Eve to come with him to the stable to see the oxen kneel before the Christ child, he would go along, " hoping it might be so."

Later in the article, Matthews returns to the Christian history for a way of setting the stage for news even as he places it beyond reach.

The only big news, private and public, that human beings are really concerned about is news of life and death. There has been no new news on either subject for some time — nearly two thousand years, in fact. The resurrection was tremendous good news if true, the best news ever reported. But though it has been told wherever Christian missionaries have gone, and a large proportion of the earth's population must have heard of it, it is still widely disbelieved or believed only in a poetic or mystical sense, as an honorable thought or an incomprehensible symbol.

So the press only reflects the world it reports and, like the world, is quite unable to recognize or accept really good news — " a saint for the ages, a lasting hero, a revelation of permanent truth; it can only exaggerate or minimize, ignore, misreport, or doubt, just like the rest of us." Thus the press must rely largely on snippets and entertainment.

What Matthews has told us is substantially the same as what Auden has said: the press and the news-reporting media exist largely to help men form the proper opinion for the time of the year. What Matthews points to as the last " new news," the story of a birth and a resurrection, constitutes the basis of the Improper Opinion, the paradox out of which the Christian faith and life are born. I do not live in such a dreamworld as to expect that someday mass media will begin reporting Bethlehems and Calvarys as the " good big news " of our time, though some coyly but reverently do it at Christmas or Easter when they seek to make the faith relevant by reporting the ancient events as contemporary.

Instead, there is the chance that in the smaller news, both good and bad, on which mass media largely exist, the Christian big news comes through. It should be possible to pull at any strand of saintliness, heroism, or common activity presented as an aspect of the Christian faith and to pull it until one comes back to the central knot: the incarnation and/or atonement. The lives portrayed should show that they are living corollaries of the doctrine of the forgiveness of sins and that all radiates from that glowing center.

This should be the generative witness of Protestantism, but precious little of it is reflected in mass-medial coverage of Protestant affairs. There is often a patronizing implication in the regard of the press for Protestantism in America. Here is an entity too large to be bypassed, too near to be summarized, too complex to be treated fairly, too ordinary to make news.

This fact creates problems for understanding people who report on religious news. Among the more perceptive in this fraternity are my colleagues as religious reporters, David Meade, of *The Chicago Daily News,* and Richard Philbrick, of the Chicago *Tribune.* Each has told me what I have observed also in others: that metropolitan newspaper church editors are less interested in gathering " snippets " for columns on religious notes and news than they are in observing the impact religion makes on the larger culture and society. They want to see it make its own way also on other than the religion pages. For anyone who takes this approach, Protestantism presents several special problems. In columns of notes and news there will always be an abundance of additions to buildings, bigger budgets, church dinners. By the abundance and variety of these it will look as if Protestantism is being given decisive coverage. If the reporter looks less for such manufactured news, exaggerated chitchat, or rumor than he does for elaborations on big good news, he comes up against perplexities.

First is Protestantism's relative lack of symbolism. Here both Roman Catholicism and Judaism have an advantage that Protestantism could develop in part only at loss to other factors that it holds dear. The mass media must rely on color, sight, sound, and circumstance for effect. The clothes of ritual and the trappings of tradition are excellent for photography and they can, wordlessly, telegraph meanings to an audience. Protestantism, in this respect, tends to wear a business suit and is in this sense less useful and imaginative to the producers and communicators to masses.

What a liability this lack of symbolism is was brought forcefully home to me some years ago when I was on a denominational committee charged with preparing a script for a motion picture that would be screened in commercial theaters, not as a religious film but as one with an implied Christian message. At the end of the film a rather minor character was to emerge as a heroic but still thoroughly human figure. Somehow the suggestion was to be planted in the viewers' minds that he was acting out of Christian motivation, but there was to be no preaching, no verbalizing. Had we desired to portray Roman Catholicism, there would have been little difficulty. The numerous sacramentals, the many little signs and symbols of the common public life — these can be telegraphed quite simply and without artificiality. I have no doubt that this obvious symbolism accounts as much for the predominance of Catholic interest in secular films as does play for power, though Protestants often suggest the contrary.

As our committee sessions wore on, suggestions ranged from the banal to the wearily absurd. To place a New Testament or a whole Bible into the character's hand (it seemed to be the only object that Protestants regard with the awe Catholics show sacramentals) would have been contrary to the normal appearance of one in his occupation. To have the camera range across the living quarters and just fall on Sallmann's *Head of Christ*, let us say, would have been thoroughly contrived. Someone suggested that among his papers, as the character leafed through them, could be a certificate, yellowed with age, of his promotion to the intermediate Sunday school of his old home town! The motion picture, sad to say, was never produced, so I can describe no solution.

A more public illustration occurred in late winter of 1959, when Detroit had two events of religious significance on the same day. One involved the elevation of the head of the Roman Catholic diocese; the other, the visit to the city by the Rev. Edwin T. Dahlberg, President of the National Council of the Churches of Christ in the U.S.A. *The Detroit News'* religion editor, Adrian Fuller, being an enterprising and fair-minded person in quest of "what makes news," saw to it that the two events received comparable coverage. The Roman Catholic event was, from the viewpoint of content, definitely secondary. But the pageantry, the prostration of clerics before the altar — all this conspired to render the event photogenic. Mr. Fuller saw to it that each of the hundreds of inches devoted to the Roman prelate was matched by equal space on the Protestant event, which involved some speechmaking and opinion-forming. The net result: a rare achievement in granting "equal time," but Protestantism was again seriously upstaged. We can bewail what Puritanism has done in putting us in lecture halls and business suits; whether we wish to retrace our steps enough to be newsworthy is an entirely different question.

In a second direction, Protestantism's problem is more serious, and this one is of its own making or at least belongs, alas, to its genius. Although Judaism is broken up into many emphases and factions, it possesses an accidental unity in its ethnic base that to anyone at any distance — say the distance the mass media provide — makes it look homogeneous and thus forceful. Roman Catholicism may be as catholic as Protestantism, as many-hued and as textured. But it possesses a single authority and is inclusive in its power structure. The concentrations of the Roman Catholic minority are consistently in the major urban centers. These are precisely the centers of mass communications. Thus anyone in upstate New York, downstate

Illinois, or around-state Maryland will, even in a region of Protestant majority, be inundated with Roman Catholic news because of Catholicism's power structure. The death of an archbishop or the elevation of a prelate to the cardinalate in New York or Chicago receives coverage exceeded — if at all — only by that given the death or inauguration of a President. As with symbolism, so with power — Protestants may not want to pay the price of a more massive appearance. But this again goes a long distance to explain the disproportion in news-reporting.

A third factor was hinted at in the second, but can now be isolated. This is the fact of New York City, home of most book publishers, magazine firms, several decisive newspapers, and a significant concentration of radio-television and advertising centers. Seventy per cent of America's magazines that have a circulation of over two hundred thousand are published in New York. Thus, although New York is not the U.S.A., as the saying goes, it has more to say about the proper opinions of the U.S.A. than any other comparable city or than any other combination of metropolitan areas (only Hollywood as a motion-picture capital prevents a New York monopoly of all communication media).

New York is made up of two million five hundred thousand Jews, about two million Roman Catholics, and one million Protestants. This population picture creates an optical illusion that this is what America is really like, and it is an understandable explanation of why America's majority religion receives such fainthearted attention in mass communications. Considerations of personal faith and consolidations of power entirely aside, it is logical that these people whose values are determined by the New York urban complex would reflect their impression. The power elites that dominate the industries are not unmindful of their non-New York markets. They may tailor much of their production for the Bible belt and the Protestant hinterlands. But it is only natural that when they look for the really decisive they look in New York's mirrors.

An example of this effect occurred in the February, 1960, issue of *Fortune* magazine, which was entirely devoted to New York City. The editorial introduction discussed the question of New York's coherence: how could an urban mass of so many millions hold together? Its answer: paradoxically, much of the glue of this secular headquarters town was religion or, rather, three religions. After paying tribute to the Protestant past and casting a glance at the Protestant present (most of New York's civic leadership is Protestant; eighteen Protestant denominations headquarter there), the magazine gets down to business and shows New York for what it is. A nine-page article describes with great taste and character "The Jewish *Élan*," and then follows an equal and even more colorful number of pages on "The Cardinal" and his archdiocese. New York, of course, is not alone. Chicago's archdiocese of more than 1.8 million Roman Catholics naturally determines the market and the setting for the second city's mass communications. There, of course, a larger Protestant remnant is active (proportionately) and the Jewish community is proportionately smaller. None of this, written by a Protestant, is said by way of complaint. It is, rather, a description of the part geography and power play in decision-making and is actually a contribution toward lessening of tensions: often Protestants imply that a conspiracy keeps them out of proper coverage.

The fourth factor in the Protestant imbalance is the liability that goes with its asset as America's dominant religion. Evangelical Christianity had so decisive a part in shaping the nation's life and manners and was in turn so decisively molded by that environment that it tends to form the background for other experiences today. Americans of various religious loyalties tend to define themselves over against Protestantism, so that Protestantism is the wallpaper into which the colorless religious events are blurred and against which the colorful stand out. So secure is it in the bedrock mores of America that it is taken for granted. It is exposed on all fronts: there is little mystery about it.

Thus it is that when the mass communications media assemble many voices from many rooms to speak on religion, the representatives of Roman Catholicism or Judaism — or, for that matter, of the colorful Protestant " sects " — will seem to speak with a different kind of authority. It is as if the burden of proof for legitimacy is theirs and this creates a certain urgency. What is more, since their theological resources are not so exposed and familiar in the national ethos as are those, say, of Presbyterianism or Congregationalism, they seem to dispense treasures of an oracular character and arcane wisdom. Observe the audience of any such gathering, and you will see expectations raised when the rabbi or priest speaks. But the Protestant is normally expected to present platitudes and pleasant affirmations.

Happy exceptions do exist and they are increasing. Now that Americans are realizing that their pluralism and Protestantism as a power thrust is losing its singular place, there is a growing distance between ethos and theology. Protestantism here will have to pay the price of easy confidence and overfamiliarity with America's ear. But it may gain the asset of standing just far enough from the judgments and proper opinions of the society that its word of judgment will be heard again as a word partly from beyond and not only from within, as a word of grace spoken in the name of a God whose goodness is not exhausted by what is apparent in temporal schemes.

Only in this connection do we plan to dwell on the tactical problems of one branch of Christianity, but such an emphasis is in place in any larger discussion of strategy. If the *marturia, leitourgia,* and *diakonia* of Protestantism are to be publicized, they must:

(*a*) exist, and be consistent with classic Christian service;

(*b*) be noticeable, but not blatant, for this would be to deny the Christian framework — it would amount again to gaining the world and losing the " soul ";

(*c*) be noticed; they must be near enough to the men who determine what news shall be reported;

(*d*) somehow be capable of symbolic representation; for in their shades of gray and their "blah" character, newsmen are as hard put to dramatize them as dramatists are to find them newsworthy.

It may be that Protestantism cannot suggest richer symbolism without losing its character; that it will prefer its state of division to a state of reportable coherence; that it will see no need for ministering to those who make decisions in the communications field; that it will not want to extricate itself in part from its environment so that it can speak to that environment and not just about it. Indeed, perhaps Protestantism will want to stay exactly where it is. But if, then, it fails to capture the imagination, it cannot complain.

Only as Protestantism suggests some of the color and richness of life (without pomp or ritual, to be sure); as it finds its unity; as it ministers to men of high station in the opinion field as well as to low; as it judges and saves its contemporaries: only to this extent can it expect imagination to be directed to it, the imagination it only too readily permits "the children of darkness" in the media fields to pre-empt. For they may be, in disguise, the children of light come to judge those who have let the big good news about life and death look like what C. S. Lewis calls "the Same Old Thing."

Chapter VI

The Content of the Presentation

"The typical American today is, in fact, a Calvinist with neither fear of hell nor hope for heaven."

This comment by Norman Birnbaum sets the stage for our discussion of the content of the Christian presentation today. Mr. Birnbaum is too sophisticated in his agnostic position, I believe, to be twitting Christians for the linguistic and conceptual changes that time has brought. By that I mean, he is probably not engaging in the kind of criticism of the faith that we used to associate with H. L. Mencken or Clarence Darrow or other latter-day opponents of the churches. They seemed to regret that Christians talked less and less in terms of pearly gates and alabaster palaces above and still less and less about flames of fire down below. For them, it was important to find someone they could expose as a fossil, a vestige of an earlier civilization — a William Jennings Bryan, for instance — who in his simple defense of the faith was willing to remythologize Christian theology with pictures of the past and future that belonged more to nineteenth-century apology than to Biblical intention in the first place.

No, more likely Mr. Birnbaum is pointing to what many thoughtful people within the churches have to observe. First, Americans in their typicality are Calvinist. This could hardly refer to an informed acquaintance with John Calvin. Rather, it points to a transformed historical reality. Calvinism, the religion that nurtured much of the American ethos, persists even

131

in secularized forms today. There is some sense of meaning in the historical process, some guidance of a providence, if you will. There is a determinacy about life that we have been calling "religion" but, without theonomous reference, is as far from historic Calvinism as it is from other forms of Christianity.

But this transformed Calvinism has accounted for some of the paradoxes of our way of life. As America grows more secular it finds a greater compulsion to speak in religious terms to justify its way of life and to soothe anxieties. Despite the relaxation of discipline on all fronts, we are still conscience-bound. Despite the freedom we have known in the political sense, we are conscious of being bound to certain courses of action as if they are predestined. So our first impulses are religious.

However, this religion is expressed within a narrow and certainly circumscribed context. It lacks the historic breadth and depth that Christian symbol attaches to "fear of hell" and "hope for heaven." Where once an eternal suffering or annihilation was seen to await the person who was not righteous before God, now the payment for penalties in the religious sense is not only confined to a vision of the here-and-now but is situation-inflicted or self-inflicted. One gets ulcers or neuroses; he is frustrated or anxious or unsuccessful. His status does not improve or his wife leaves him — this is hell, or at least the only hell he fears. And whatever orthodox theologies in Catholicism or Protestantism alike profess, Americans in their averageness — committed to these faiths or not — reveal quite clearly that hope of heaven is now symbolically contained in the middle-class paradise. It may mean suburbia; it may mean status or security. But it is again confined, circumscribed, and of one's own making.

Whether Christians confront religious America (or secular America), then, in a faith rich in imagery and filled with sign-posts of symbolic and designatory value or whether they prepare a demythologized but intentionally faithful modern version, they will speak en masse to insulated people. This is not new, and a false impression would be created if I suggested that some sense of discovery motivates me. But the nature of the insulation changes in every age. And mass media have had their part in changing that nature in our own time. Birnbaum's poles of thought will provide the paradigm under which the content of the Christian presentation can be discussed. Each can be condensed under the abstractions "judgment" and "grace" (though countless other terms would do).

The presence of this dialectic in Biblical discourse needs no elaboration. "The time is fulfilled, and the kingdom of God is at hand; repent, and believe in the gospel." (Mark 1:14.) "For the law was given through Moses; grace and truth came through Jesus Christ." (John 1:17.) "Wretched man that I am! Who will deliver me from this body of death? Thanks be to God through Jesus Christ our Lord!" (Rom. 7:24–25.) "For I through the law died to the law, that I might live to God." (Gal. 2:19.)

We may dwell a moment on Pauline thought where the distinction is consistent. Paul speaks a great deal of the wrath of God and consistently counters this with the affirmation that Christ rescues us from the wrath which is to come (I Thess. 1:10). The law remains to judge, and God's demand is constant; grace is not a charter for license. As a Hebrew of the Hebrews, Paul's whole memory is surrounded by the comfort the law had given him, the security it once held. But that is removed as time goes by: "I died under the law." Although repentance plays a relatively minor role in his thought, he does point to the limits of the way of the law and the need for a turn to the viewpoint of faith. When he speaks of turning, however (Phil. 3:7), he gives up the law that had been his pride. And the attempt to gain salvation by fulfilling the law is doomed. "So that no human being might boast in the presence of God." (I Cor. 1:29.) Christ, who is appropriated through faith, is the end of the law and of human glorying (Rom. 10:4). Both judgment and grace continue to play parts in human life, but grace is decisive for a Christian:

Christ the end of the law! That means, then, that he is the end of a life, which, sustained by the need for recognition (implying secret dread and hatred of God), seeks to establish its own righteousness. Christ is the end of the law as the end of sin, self-glorying, and reliance on the flesh: he is the end of the law as the way of salvation; he is the means of access to the way of salvation through grace for the true believer, that is, for the man who gives up his own righteousness and surrenders himself completely to the God who leads man from death into life.[22]

No Christian name is more associated with the judgment/ grace distinction than is that of Augustine, who has provided the setting of most later dialogue for a millennium because of the ways in which he fought off Pelagianism in the name of Paulinism. He made much of the judgment that comes upon man because of the Fall, which was motivated by pride. Human nature was seminally present in its totality in the first man, Adam. " As a personal act, the first sin was not our act but the act of another; yet it was truly the common act of mankind in their collective or undistributed form of existence."

As God's judgment falls upon the sinful human race, man is restored only through grace. It attaches itself to the vestige of the divine image. Love is infused. Man is justified, renovated, made holy (he makes little distinction between being justified and being sanctified) in the grace that is in Christ Jesus.

In classic Roman Catholic thought, notably in Thomas Aquinas, there is a further development that includes some blending of judgment and grace, but the two make up the Christian content. Judgment comes through the laws: " the natural law, the law of lust, the Mosaic law, and the gospel law " (*sic*). The last is the law of love, of Christ and his gospel. (*De Duobus Praeceptis Caritatis, I.*) Grace is a created, divine, and supernatural power through which far beyond proper expectations human nature is fulfilled. Man is, in a sense, deified as he participates in the divine life and nature and he can then accomplish deeds of a supernatural character. Man is a form that can be filled with a higher potentiality, which grace represents as an infinite stream of love, the new *erōs*, the new fullness of God (Karl Adam). Grace according to Aquinas, is a "sort of perfection which elevates the soul to some supernatural existence."

With the Protestant Reformation the two terms are kept and the distinction is radically sharpened. As a matter of fact, Martin Luther made the discrimination between the two decisive in determining Christian theologians' capabilities. For him "law" and "gospel" pointed to these realities. God encounters man through both. God confronts us as the sovereign Lord who must judge the transgressor; he asks for obedience. But man has fallen, completely. In contrast to Catholicism, Reformation thought did not permit one to speak of judgment directed only to an impaired but somehow intact good nature. Man is cut off from God by judgment, which is an alien work of the Deity.

The proper work of God counters all proper human expectations. Grace comes in the unexpected form, a gift in Jesus Christ. The law annihilated all human claims; the gift of grace completely effected a new reality in man. The plan for man is totally changed in the Christ-event.

Reformed Christianity, whether Calvinist or Arminian in bent, affirms that God both judges and heals and that the proclamation is not whole and full unless both acts are present. But from different angles there are new parallels emergent to Roman Catholic theology in the sense of blurring the two. Calvin was as concerned as Luther to distinguish between law and gospel but the distinction is purely formal. Judgment is not a strange or foreign work of God. Rather, law and gospel are two stages of revelation that complement each other: "The gospel has not succeeded the whole law, so as to introduce a different way of salvation; but rather to confirm and ratify the promises of the law, and to connect the body with the shadows."[23]

The arguments over the radical character of each, as well as the relative distinction, persist with many shadings; each way

of separating or joining the two concepts and realities determines the character of the whole theology. But the point that
is clear from extensions of these inquiries is this: Christian
proclamation that is antinomian in nature, totally rejecting the
power of the judgment of God, is partial; and proclamation that
is legalistic in its decisive stance, not allowing the break-
through of grace, is not Christian. There is a double-sidedness
in divine revelation and God's relation to man; both sides must
find expression also in the mass media of communication if we
are interested in the fullness of the Christian faith. As we explore how these are presented, it becomes more obvious why
implicit expression does more justice to the medium than explicit denunciation or therapy.

The delineations may be brief. Nonreligious, secular, or
" worldly " judgment via mass communications may be termed
" preprophetic." Its context is, from the Christian point of view,
limited, for it lacks the dimension that the absolutely taut Biblical conception of the wrath of God provides. Yet it lays the
groundwork for Biblically oriented analysis and as such is often
warmly welcomed by perceptive churchmen. This attempt to
utter judgment concerning man's condition short of reference
to the God of Biblical faith is well-defined in the phrase " tragic
sense of life." It is analytic but does not necessarily point the
way to therapy. It offers realism without redemption, which,
from the Christian point of view, is still preferable to the offer
of sentimentality and illusory redemption. This approach is
nearly normative in the " pathetic " or the tragic strain of modern literature that often finds its way into mass communications,
as in the work, for example, of Eugene O'Neill, Arthur Miller,
William Inge, and other dramatists and script-writers. This
strain invokes a fear of hell, though it acknowledges no hell
beyond the entrapment and futility of man's present condition.

Secondly, we might speak of normally religious use of mass
communications in the aspect of judgment as the " prophetic "
attempt. Here again we encounter explicit denunciation, effective in the redemptive circle but ineffective with a mass audi-

ence that has moved beyond the God of religious faith. At its
best it lacks art. We might say here of negation what Amos
Wilder says of affirmation:

> The affirmation in art is properly implicit rather than explicit.
> The poet is an image maker rather than a preacher, a celebrant
> rather than a teacher. It is true that poetry and religion are
> consubstantial in their origins. The poet, at the risk of being a
> magician in the bad sense, cannot finally be distinguished from
> the seer and prophet. Yet the poet ministers to true belief and
> right conduct, not by indoctrination or didactic, but by en-
> abling us to *see* — in the sense that Goethe ascribed to it:
> *schauen*.[24]

The prophet as denouncer in indiscriminate utterance of God's
judgments to mass audiences who do not believe in the God of
whom he speaks, therefore, does not even use his art to minister
to " right conduct." He may actually be complicating the task of
Christian missions. So if at its best the explicit form of judgment
lacks art, at its worst it caricatures the Biblical conception of
the wrath of God.

The Christian pronouncement of judgment therefore must be
" postprophetic," in many ways allied with the " pathetic " or
tragic sense of life in the modern world. Yet it tantalizes, it
teases, it insinuates, a better prospect. It suggests to people who
have gone beyond religion in determining patterns of conduct
that although religious moralism is not an option for them, the
God of the Christian faith is. Further, it suggests that the Christian faith reintroduces into life a sanity and a basis that can
come only because the demand of a living God is uncompromis-
ing, taut, unyielding. This approach, finding a kinship with the
secular at its best, opens the door for a fuller witness to the
Christian faith. Its method, therefore, is implicit. It fuses art
with discretion; it cares about the world and shows this by the
way it tells its story. It does not assume that a mass audience
will feel judged by reference to a God in whom it does not believe. Its attitude is akin, not to that of Jonah (the religious
prophet who despises Nineveh in the name of God), but that of

Jesus, who loved the city over which he wept and in which he died and rose. Similarly, the postprophetic insinuation was clear in Jesus' judgment of the woman at the well in Samaria (John, ch. 4), whom he did not alienate by premature prideful exclusion.

The same somewhat chronological sequence can now be applied to the therapeutic approach to a world that has, even in its religion, moved beyond God. Here we see a "postevangelical" assumption in the highest positive popular art, the non-Christian, nonreligious literature of affirmation. This is the good news that operates entirely within the context of the human situation and which, although it is limited from the Christian viewpoint, at least begins to provide courage and hope. God is dead. Yet men live on. Albert Camus was the most noted figure for this affirmative element in modern literature, but his kind of emphasis predominated also in most of the movies issued during wartime, as typified later in *The Diary of Anne Frank.* She, who best knew what men were like at their worst, was sure "at the end" that basically, in spite of all, men were good. This is the evangelical note wherever hope persists outside of hope in Jesus Christ. It is of some use to Christians, who find in it at least a better alternative than sentimentality or despair.

The second presentation of therapy is the explicitly "evangelical," which, although it may have specific Christian orientation, necessarily is regarded "religiously" by the mass audience. It fails in that it assumes a covenanted community but actually lacks one. It possesses all the words but none of the music of God's healing promises to a chosen, responsive, respondible people. In its religious context it unwittingly offers grace without judgment; sometimes wittingly it does so, as in the evangelical promise of positive thought without particular reference to Jesus Christ.

The most salutary function of mass communications for telling the healing and reconciling story, from the Christian point of view, might properly be termed "pre-evangelical." This is not intended as a simple translation of that *praeparatio evan-*

gelica which serves as bridge between the religions and Christian faith. It may be much more theologically and philosophically naïve than all that. It merely prepares the soil. It intrigues and raises curiosity. Not ashamed of the gospel of Christ, it participates sufficiently in the agonies of human existence on the path to salvation to speak realistically to the world, and avoids cheap grace in the church. It has room for the Improper Opinion, but it whispers rather than shouts. Its employment serves to attract people who would overhear a whisper but who would yawn at a shout about "the same old thing." It avoids pat verbalizing of the gospel and avoids extensive systematic presentation of the good news, leaving that for the proclaimers of the Word within the Christian community who profit from this preparation. Any telling of a good story about the Christian life contributes to this effect.

It is in this final place that mass communications can best serve a church alert to their subtleties. This is the heart of the story, when Jesus Christ, who took the form of a servant, can be presented in the humility, obscurity, and hidden glory of Christian lives. When this occurs, the mass media are what the arts can be: *ancillae*, handmaidens to the Word of God. The revelation that develops is one of partial concealment; but the mask of the media can lead people to the disciplined, covenanted, worshiping community where more of the fullness appears in the uncompromised evangelical proclamation.

This "pre-evangelical" emphasis implies a Word in the verbal sense just as it points to the Word in the incarnate Lord. But to an audience that has moved beyond God into secularity or self-serving religiosity, its indirect and implicit witness prepares people whose ears have been closed — through action, perhaps without a word. The New Testament is crowded with this emphasis; it is confined not at all to the "See how they love one another!" motif. It is classically stated in The First Letter of Peter, written to a diasporate situation such as the one the church knows today: "Likewise you wives, be submissive to your husbands, so that some, though they do not obey the word,

may be won without a word by the behavior of their wives"
(I Peter 3:1).

"Though they do not obey the word": this is the postprophetic situation; "may be won without a word": this is the
pre-evangelical. It is the familiar story of Jesus Christ presented
through lives, actions, and story so effectively that a world —
including one of mass communicators — cannot fail to take
note. The follow-up activity of the Christian community is then
simplified, not complicated as now it is so often by the mis-
understood judgment and misapplied grace of merely religious
mass communication.

Conclusion: What Do We Do?

1. The Christian churches in a world significantly shaped by mass media of communication begin by analysis and interpretation; it is impossible to minister without having some sort of theological construct in which the media can be appraised.

2. They will find that for the most part they have more at stake in the frankly secular, than in the religious, use of the media, whether under specifically Christian or under more generalized religious auspices. This will be clear in the varieties of ways in which the "preprophetic" judgment parallels and offers an avenue to Biblical witness just as "postevangelical" promise provides an open door to the authentic gospel. Religious communication often lacks the seriousness of each of these dimensions and seeks to achieve in a mass audience what can only be effectively nurtured within the Christian cultus.

3. Since religious and Christian use of mass communications will represent a minority situation in a world like ours, it is important that the churches go about their first business, taking on "the form of a servant" and presenting Christ through this mask or in this image rather than through noisy self-advertisement.

4. Normally, implicit judgment and preparation for the gospel will be more effective to a mass audience than will blatant, premature verbalization or formulization of law-and-gospel slogans, as incomprehensible and dismissable as the latter are beyond the Christian community.

5. By being the kind of church whose story mass communicators cannot avoid: in its stand for social justice, racial equality, political liberty; in the quieter works of love; in the pleasing countenance of the Lord in whose image it is born, the church can survive and see its call enhanced in the modern world that has not lost — it has only *apparently* lost — its need for the Christian gospel. Only in such an instance, when its story so improves, will it come to life outside the " graveyard " hours of radio and television and off the back pages to the " prime time " and the front pages it will only then again deserve.

This leaves, does it not, something for all Christians to *do* about the world of proper opinions where the Improper Opinion concerning God's activity in Jesus Christ never " fits in " but in which it still attracts and saves?

Notes

1. C. S. Lewis, *The Screwtape Letters* (Collins Fontana Books edition, London, 1956), p. 126.

2. Robert Sarnoff, in *Safety in the 60's* (National Safety Council, 1959), p. 126. Many of the statistics of the extent of media are taken from Wilbur Schramm, *Responsibility in Mass Communication* (Harper & Brothers, 1957), p. 30.

3. Yves M. J. Congar, O. P., *Lay People in the Church*, translated by Donald Attwater (The Newman Press, 1957), pp. 98–100.

4. Walter Freytag, *The Gospel and the Religions* (S.C.M. Press, Ltd., London, 1957), p. 43.

5. John Baillie, *Our Knowledge of God* (Charles Scribner's Sons, 1959), pp. 201 ff.

6. *The Journals of Sören Kierkegaard*, edited and translated by Alexander Dru (Oxford University Press, 1939), p. 633.

7. Martin Heinecken, *The Moment Before God* (Muhlenberg Press, 1956), pp. 41–42.

8. Karl Barth, *Das Wort Gottes und die Theologie*, translated by H. R. Mackintosh (1925), p. 172.

9. Paul Tillich, *Systematic Theology*, Vol. I (University of Chicago Press, 1951), pp. 56 f.

10. Tillich, *op. cit.*, Vol. II (1957), p. 92.

11. Albert Outler, "Ordeal of a Happy Dilettante," in *The Christian Century* (February 3, 1960), p. 129.

12. Doubleday Anchor Book, 1959.

13. Robert E. Park, *Race and Culture* (The Free Press of Glencoe, 1950), p. 240.

14. In *Fordham University Quarterly,* Vol. XXXIII, No. 128, Spring, 1958.

15. Göte Bergsten, *Pastoral Psychology* (George Allen & Unwin, Ltd., London, 1951), p. 75.

16. Friedrich Nietzsche, *Joyful Wisdom,* translated by Thomas Common (George Allen & Unwin, Ltd., London, 1909), sec. 125.

17. Archibald M. Hunter, *Introducing New Testament Theology* (The Westminster Press, 1957), p. 66.

18. In *Daedalus* (Summer, 1958), pp. 22 ff.

19. C. H. Dodd, *The Apostolic Preaching* (Willett, Clarke & Company, 1937), p. 8.

20. William H. Whyte, Jr., *The Organization Man* (Doubleday Anchor Book, 1957), p. 418.

21. *Atlantic* (December, 1957), pp. 80 ff., later incorporated into Matthews' book *The Sugar Pill* (Victor Gollancz, Ltd., London, 1957).

22. Rudolf Bultmann, *Essays: Philosophical and Theological,* translated by James C. G. Greig (The Macmillan Company, 1955), p. 54.

23. John Calvin, *Institutes of the Christian Religion,* translated by John Allen (Presbyterian Board of Christian Education, 1936), II. ix. 4.

24. In *Spiritual Problems in Contemporary Literature,* edited by Stanley Romaine Hopper (Harper Torchbook, 1957), p. 244.

In this book the author examines the question whether it is possible for the Christian faith to communicate, or, preferably, to " present " itself through the channels of mass media so widely and so effectively employed in the modern world.

Our culture, unlike that of the Middle Ages, is predominantly secular, and when mass media — books, magazines, newspapers, movies, radio, television — are applied within that culture, secular assumptions are inevitable. Within limits, mass media can direct and even create public reaction, but they cannot with impunity exceed those limits. They must remain within the bounds of what the secular social ethos considers " proper " opinion. They may, indeed, carry a comfortable religious undertone and still be tolerated, but not the vital stinging challenge of the gospel — not " the surprising interruption of God in Christ." That would be " improper " opinion. Yet it is precisely that improper opinion, that stumbling block or " scandal," to which the Christian church must bear witness or fail of its purpose. Are we, then, reduced to the admission that the church can make no use of mass media? Dr. Marty does not think so.